Katharine Welby-Roberts speaks and writes about issues relating to mental and emotional health, and the wider context of how the Church responds to those who are suffering. She is married to Mike and they live in Reading with their baby son Elijah. Much of her time is taken up with occupying Elijah and drinking tea with other mums but, in addition to those things, she loves a good steak, comic-book films and wine.

I Thought there would be Cake

Katharine Welby-Roberts

SPCK

First published in Great Britain in 2017

Society for Promoting Christian Knowledge
36 Causton Street
London SW1P 4ST
www.spck.org.uk

British Library Cataloguing-in-Publication Data
A catalogue record for this book is available from the British Library

ISBN 978–0–281–07576–8
eBook ISBN 978–0–281–07577–5

Typeset by Manila Typesetting Company
Manufacture managed by Jellyfish
First printed in Great Britain by CPI
Subsequently digitally printed in Great Britain

eBook by Manila Typesetting Company

Produced on paper from sustainable forests

Special thanks to Mike –
for his encouragement and love
through the storms and calm,
and to Ginny –
a hero without whom my brain would be a lot less
able to find paths through the chaos within

Contents

Introduction

Life has not turned out quite how I hoped it would. It is too hard, too full of disappointment and upset. Everything that is good seems very hard work to get. I remember as a child wishing I was a grown-up. They had it all! They had their own money, they could stay up late, watch TV or hang out with friends whenever they felt like it. They could drive, and dress up all fancy and go to parties. Basically, I idealized adulthood.

Being an adult looked to me like a party where there was shed-loads of cake. And then I grew up and was very disappointed. I found that there was a lot of other stuff and not so much cake. The thing is, much of that other stuff (the vegetables of life) is not bad for you; it is just different and not as sweet.

Over the course of this book I am going to explore some of the parts of life that have hindered me the most. These issues are like mushy, overcooked brussels sprouts – nobody wants to live with them and I certainly want to be rid of them.

It feels like a very arrogant thing to do, to write a book. Not for other people – they are wise and sensible to do so – but I am clearly not the best person to share any form of wisdom, nonsense or life experience in such a format. A book feels oddly formal – more permanent than my usual blog or article. It feels like I am stepping out into the world and saying, 'I am important, you should listen to me!' This is really not what I am aiming to do, but as I sit here thinking about writing it I cannot help but feel that this is what it will look like.

The problem is, I am very much someone who cares about what it will look like to others. I have such admiration and respect (and the odd hint of jealousy!) for people who seem able to not take to heart what others think or say of them. Those who can genuinely not be affected by the thoughts and feelings of others, to let them go, and say, 'This is who I am!' without shame, fear or apprehension about how others will react.

I do the opposite. I say, 'This is who I am!' and then, if I suspect that someone is thinking that 'what I am' is not good enough, or irritating or stupid, I wonder if perhaps I announced too soon. This begs the question – why would anyone who is so unsure of themselves that they depend on the opinions of others to define themselves, ever think that writing a book on self-worth was a good idea?

I am writing this Introduction while I am still about halfway through the rest of the book, and I really can't answer this question. I am at a point in the process where I honestly don't know why I started. I clearly don't think terribly much of myself. I am riddled with issues of self-doubt and fear, and am almost crippled by imposter syndrome, wondering at my arrogance at thinking I could ever write a book!

Then I remember – that was sort of the point.

I am not writing a book of answers, if that is what you were hoping for. I am writing a book exploring self-worth, pondering what it would mean to resign yourself to the fact that you are who you are, and even to enjoy it just a little. Perhaps even to dare to start to love yourself – not in an 'I am awesome', arrogant, clearly hiding a few issues sort of way, but in a quiet, reflective acknowledgement that what you are is enough to make you lovable. To make you acceptable. To be worthy of care and attention.

I have never really believed these things to be true, but I don't think it is right to believe them not to be true. I do believe in God, and therefore in what the Bible says. However, the Bible contradicts almost everything I say about myself. It says I am worthy of love; it says I am unique and valuable. It says I am of incomparable value to God.

If I believe in God, and believe what he says, then I must start to believe this of myself. However, how do you change a lifetime of habits of believing that you are the opposite of all these things?

Through this book, I will jump into some of my greatest issues, and try to explore how I can change my patterns of thinking. Despite my long-held belief that I am alone in thinking how I do, I have been reliably informed that, apparently, the issues I deal with are common to many of us.

My hope is that as I learn how to put some of my thinking into perspective, as I journey through the deepest, darkest parts of my self-doubt, I might begin to accept that there is value to my existence. That there is hope, and that I am worthy of love and even self-love. And, despite using myself as an example, I hope that this book offers you a chance to journey with me, to explore where some of these issues need to be dug into for yourself. I want to open up the possibility that we have bought into the lie that society so often tells us – that we will never be enough – and that we can begin to believe that it just might not be true.

It seems that the world doesn't want us to think that what we are is OK. In most self-help literature, and in advertising, for example, we are led to believe that we are *almost* OK. If we do this one thing, make this one change, if we try this, or think that, then we will become better. We will become acceptable.

My experience is that a lot of Christian literature is the same. While it is often brilliant and challenging – and it is not a bad thing to explore how we might grow – the problem comes when we believe that to be OK, loved and considered acceptable, we must first change.

The intention may not be to say that, but it is the impression I get. To be 'better' I must pray more often, engage further with God, read the Bible more. And probably buy that phone, drive that car, wear those clothes. I should eat a better diet, exercise more, think positive thoughts. I must 'do' something in order to be OK.

I really don't want this book to suggest that you need to do anything. Rather, I want to explore the possibility that what you are, right now, is enough. Yes, there might be room for growth and change throughout your life. However, in this exact moment, what I am is enough to make me acceptable, loved, cherished and valued. What I bring to this world is good; I am unique and essentially so.

I was once told that the only thing that grows in a day is a mushroom. Whether or not that is true, I quite like the imagery. I don't want to be a mushroom.

If you looked at an acorn, no one would be likely to say, 'Stupid acorn, why are you not an oak? You clearly have not tried hard enough!' It is an accepted fact that an acorn takes years to become a fully grown tree. Similarly, why do we expect ourselves to be fully grown, perfect and 'as we should be', not allowing ourselves to take time to develop? I would rather spend a lifetime learning, growing and accepting where I am on the journey than become a mushroom and expect to be complete in a day.

This book doesn't offer answers. It is my journey into learning that perhaps my existence is not some unhappy accident that I just have to make the best of. By the end, I don't think I will come out skipping and singing my praises, but I hope that I will have reached a place where I am nearer to accepting who I am.

I want to explore a strategy to manage and process certain issues – ways to live with them and start to move out of them. There is no instant fix but the slow and steady growth, like an acorn, that comes from a healthy appreciation of myself, based in humility rather than shame.

I hope that this will be a helpful and gentle journey you can participate in. I am not asking for affirmation, or for encouragement. I am writing this because I am tired of believing the lie that I have to be more than I am to be OK, and tired of the conversations with my friends who believe the same.

Not all the issues I explore will apply to you, but for those that do, I hope that you can journey with me and explore the reality that they exist in your life, what may have led to those beliefs, and what might lead you into a truer way of thinking. Hopefully, you might start to believe that you are valuable as you are.

1 Taking responsibility

I am assuming that most people have, at some point, heard that failure is a good thing. It's the whole 'if Thomas Edison had given up after the first failure we would all be living in darkness' story – the one that's told again and again to illustrate the importance of failure. Thomas Edison was an American inventor and businessman. In fact, according to his Wikipedia page (because Wikipedia is *never* wrong), he has been called America's greatest inventor. He invented the light bulb.

The story goes that as an inventor he was a really good 'tryer' – someone unafraid to fail. He tried over and over to get it right – 10,000 times apparently – and finally he succeeded and ta-da! Let there be light!

OK, so not quite. He didn't invent the light bulb, he improved on an invention that was already out there, and someone else would have succeeded if he had failed. But the story is usually told as a testimony to the importance of failure, and it cannot be denied that if he hadn't been willing to fail he wouldn't have become known throughout the world. Our failures and flaws help us to grow and learn. Through them we find out what works and what doesn't. If we have no fear of failure we can be creative, innovative and bold in our life choices.

Other popular examples include Richard Branson, who apparently liked to hear that his children had failed at something every day, as it meant that they had been taken out of their comfort zone. And the guy who invented WD-40, apparently so named because it was his fortieth attempt to get the formula right.

I have come across speakers and writers who are so brilliant at describing the kind of life you can lead if you don't fear failure that I start to believe that I could do anything. I would be a vet, or a doctor, an internationally bestselling novelist, probably be able to sing and act too.

My mind gets carried away with the excitement and sense of adventure a whole world of failure would bring me. Then I remember – I am TERRIFIED of failure.

I hate to be seen as wrong. I hate to be seen as silly or foolish. I am determined to accomplish great things and I am filled with shame at the slightest hint of anything going wrong. Now, I am not saying that if I did accept failure I would become the above bizarre combination of careers and skills, but I am fairly sure that I would not give up and run away – or get so angry – as often as I do.

In reality, I am not actually scared of getting stuff wrong. I believe those who say that getting stuff wrong is part of the journey. The aspect of failure that causes me to run away is when other people realize that I don't know what I am doing or saying.

It is other people – those who have the opportunity to point and laugh – that make failure so scary. I used to write blogs regularly, but not so much now largely because I am afraid of what people will say. I want to comment on news and current events, to write and think about things beyond my own mental health, but I am terrified of saying the wrong thing and having people tell me that I am stupid.

Most of my blogs are about me, my mental health and how I feel, and when I talk about myself no one can really say that I am wrong or stupid. However, I once wrote a more theological post and someone commented, 'You should probably do a theology degree before you try to get into this!' Actually, I *do* have a theology degree. But that showed me that I shouldn't try to go beyond talking about myself. Putting yourself in a position where you can be told you are wrong, or you can fail at something you want to succeed at, leaves you vulnerable to unkind comments and responses.

Other people don't just make failure scary, they make any acknowledgement of wrongdoing scary. In any situation where it could clearly be stated that I am not a 'success', or a 'perfect' sort of person, I start to react and respond defensively.

Whenever there is a hint that I might be wrong, I struggle to acknowledge that fact. Admitting that I have failed, or been unkind, is to my mind akin to admitting that I am a boring, fraudulent failure who will never accomplish anything and should live alone until the day I die.

Just last week, I loaded the dishwasher (which I don't do that often). This is usually my husband Mike's job – apparently only he knows how to do it correctly. But as his love language is acts of service, and for once I had the energy to do it, I thought I would help out. I was proud of my dishwasher loading; it looked tidy and sensibly done. Then he came into the kitchen and, without acknowledging my skills, rearranged two chopping boards. I started to get angry – my husband, through that demonstration of his dishwasher-loading superiority, was clearly informing me that he thought I was stupid and useless.

I mean, who can argue against that logic? I got cross, and this led to half an hour of arguing over dishwasher-loading etiquette (seriously!). We then established that I was possibly overreacting and he would in future say thank you before rearranging chopping boards. This is just one example of the way I tend to respond to any indication that I might not have done something perfectly.

I sort of pride myself on my ability to acknowledge wrong-doing – I can recognize when I have been rude to someone, or unkind. Logically I know I should apologize, regardless of any provocation on the other person's part – but it really isn't that simple. Because if I acknowledge that I have done something wrong then I will have been proven to be a fool – someone not worth knowing.

The irrational part of my brain goes 'Yes, but . . .', and I just can't do it. This is my thinking: 'I cannot say that really I shouldn't have snapped at you. I wouldn't have if you had been nicer to me. I can't take all the responsibility for my behaviour. You caused me to behave in the way I did. Before we get to the apology thing, you should acknowledge that it was all your fault. Then I will look good and gracious, apologizing for reacting badly when to be honest anyone would have done the same.'

Going back to the dishwasher, this is exactly how we concluded. I said sorry for getting so worked up over the chopping boards, but only after Mike had apologized for not saying thank you to me for loading the dishwasher in the first place.

And yet, I walked away – as I so often do – feeling guilty that I had not taken more responsibility for my actions. No matter how aware I am that I behave in this way, I can't help it. I panic. I realize that I have failed or am not perfect, and that people will see just how much of a fraud I am and walk away.

I have noticed that I can apologize to strangers, or casual acquaintances – people who are less significant in the grand scheme of my life, and it doesn't matter whether they like me or not – more easily than to family and friends.

I am a pro at pointing out flaws in others, but when it comes to acknowledging them in myself and working through them, I just try to hide away. I put up a spiky shield and challenge anyone to point out the bad behaviour in me.

I am describing two different things here: my fear of failure is what leads me to fear being shown to be in the wrong. They feel the same to me but they are not. For example, hurting someone, or lying, things that I know are wrong, are very different from failing. With failing, my reputation is at stake (or it feels like it is). I may be at risk of embarrassment. With doing something wrong, I am causing harm to others and myself.

While the two are intertwined, I want to focus on the impact my regular refusal to acknowledge responsibility has on those I love. And, of course, on my almost permanent feelings of guilt.

This is, I have discovered, not unique to me. Many of us struggle to acknowledge our bad behaviour without providing some justification for it. There is something acutely vulnerable about owning up to being wrong; not just wrong in terms of hard facts, but wrong in that – for want of a more grown-up sort of word – we have been naughty!

The naughty part isn't what comes first, half the time. In the course of a conversation, for example, I state a fact and someone refutes it. But, you see, I *know* I am right. So I get mean, and point out where the other person is wrong; or I get plain aggressive. It's not an attractive trait, and probably the main cause of my expectation that people will not like me. Then I will dig my heels in: 'If you hadn't shown me up, I wouldn't have felt like a cornered cat and lashed out.' And I find a way of passing on responsibility to someone – anyone – else. (Poor Mike gets the worst of this side of me.)

This doesn't aid reconciliation, nor does it solve the issue that has arisen. It leaves a nasty trail of guilt, though, that will plague my mind for days (if it was only a minor thing) or even months (when I have been really naughty!).

In an attempt to think about this behaviour in a more useful light, I want to delve into the reasons that may be behind it. The fear of failure is clearly significant, and something I will come back to many times throughout the book. It causes me to be so afraid of what others think of me that I struggle to acknowledge my bad behaviour. This is what I want to explore now.

What is it that makes it so hard to own up to our bad behaviour? To acknowledge when we are wrong and to apologize without justification or excuse?

Some people are very good at owning up. I have a friend, Frank (not his real name, and this applies to all the people I mention in this book – but seriously, there should be more Franks!), who is completely unafraid of failure. I marvel at his capacity to go into any challenge, have it all go wrong and come out smiling. This also affects how he deals with his own wrongdoing in relation to other people. We were having a bit of a debate about Christian dating, and I was fed up, and said something about the men tending to treat the women without respect. He got a little defensive of his gender and made some remark about how women were too needy and just wanted someone to propose to them.

Anyone familiar with this particular debate will know how heated it can be, and I lost my temper. The truth was that both of us said things we regretted and, technically, I did start it. I am not terribly subtle and have a habit of making sweeping statements that are by no means applicable to all. But Frank, instead of digging his heels in, listened to me as I explained why what he had said was hurtful.

In that way the whole conversation cooled off. I got a chance to air my grievances and he quietly listened. Afterwards he apologized, without any sense of defensiveness, and I was rather put to shame. He wasn't alone in having behaved badly and I had provoked him. When he apologized he didn't say, 'I'm sorry – but I just felt I needed to defend my gender.' He just apologized. No 'but', and without the paralysing fear I have of acknowledging wrongdoing. He is someone with absolute confidence in himself, but that confidence is coupled with a humility that enables him to own the fact that he isn't perfect.

For those of you who struggle in the same way I do, it might be worth pausing here for a moment to think through the above questions. I find that 'what' questions are more useful than 'why' questions. 'Why did I behave that way?' often has a simple answer – I feel threatened, entitled or simply confident in my own 'rightness' on any given topic. The 'what' question requires going deeper. What is it that causes me to react in the way I do?

The 'without justification or excuse' tagged on the end of the question is, for me, quite simple. I find it practically impossible to let other people's bad behaviour slide. It feels like an injustice, so I have to point out where they have gone wrong, especially if I'm owning up too. In Frank's position I would have said, 'I am so sorry, I said some unkind things. I just felt you were being very unfair to my sex and so I lashed out.' I would have sincerely meant my apology, but it was conditional on his understanding of the fact that I wouldn't have behaved that way if he hadn't caused me to. Frank didn't do this. He let the injustice of it go in order to offer me a sincere apology, without condition. I am scared that if I do that, those I apologize to might go away thinking that they are superior to me. I can't have that!

Herein, I suppose, lies the issue. Appearing inferior to the person I am dealing with (whoever they may be) confirms all my worst fears. A conversation with a very wise woman helped me to come up with a list of reasons why I struggle to take responsibility for when I behave badly.

- Loss of control – control is good. It makes life easier. You know what is going on, and you are essentially the boss (and you are never wrong!).
- Losing reputation – the irony of this one, of course, is that those who acknowledge their wrongdoing and apologize for it are actually considered more trustworthy, and often admired for it.
- Being punished – if I am the only one to acknowledge wrongdoing then you have the power to punish me. If we are both proved to be in the wrong, then really, we should let each other off the hook. Or that's my logic.
- Being rejected, losing you, being abandoned by you, being criticized by you, being judged by you – there is something of a theme here. I want you to like me, love me and trust me. If I show you how human I am, if I acknowledge I am not perfect and not always right and justified, then you might walk away.

This last one, of being rejected, is probably my greatest fear. Up to when I was 14, I was part of a large group of friends at school.

We were going from lower school into upper school, starting GCSEs, and suddenly life felt more serious. There were probably about ten to twelve of us who had been friends since we started secondary school, and some of us from before then. During the summer holidays I didn't see much of my friends, as I was away with my family for about a month.

When we went back in September it appeared that the others had met in the holidays and had decided that I should no longer be a part of the group. I, and another girl, had been cut out. There had been a new girl in the group a year earlier, and while we had started out great friends, we fought a lot and ended up disliking each other. She was now a central part of the group, and it was the two people she didn't like who were cut out. A couple of them would chat to me in class and in the corridors, but largely when they were all together at break times and out of school I was not allowed to join in. I had to find new friends.

To be honest, I don't know how much my mind has played with that story in the intervening years. But whether or not it was planned during the holidays, I was certainly rejected, and no longer able to participate in that group of friends. I do remember very clearly the staggering sense of loneliness, betrayal and hurt I felt.

Because I was never sure what I had done wrong, this re-inforced in me the fact that I could make people abandon me, without even trying. I had always been good at making new friends – our family moved a lot when we were kids – so it didn't take me too long to adapt. However, there is nothing quite like people actively choosing to cut you out, without warning or obvious reason.

This isn't justification for my not taking responsibility when I behave badly, but it does help to explain why I fear the reaction of others.

There is a risk, when exploring in a Christian context how you feel about yourself, of getting bogged down in jargon. One standard response people give to the way I react to getting stuff wrong is that I am coming at life from an orphan spirit. A bit of Christianese there, which essentially means that I have not accepted that I am fully loved by God and been accepted as I am. I continue to live as though I have no one to love me unconditionally – like an orphan who has been adopted but continues to live as if they are parentless, having to fend and fight for themselves. But honestly, what does that mean practically? I get the theory, and feel I should find it encouraging, but it has absolutely no impact; I continue to fear being proven to be a complete failure of a human being who is well worth abandoning.

I want a practical way in which I can start to change the way I respond and react, so I will ask another question. **What is it that would make it safe to be wrong? What would make it possible to apologize without pointing to the failings in others with too much enthusiasm?**

There are two parts to the answers to this: external and internal. The external part is trusting in those who are around you, the people who love you. The internal part is trusting in the knowledge that we are totally forgiven, loved and cherished by God, and that his grace (his forgiveness and unconditional love) covers us and makes us safe.

Both aspects of this challenge me. I struggle (hence the point of this book) to understand, believe and trust that people truly love me. I might *know* they love me, but feeling it and trusting in it are two different things. In the same way I *know* that God loves me. I have read the Bible and believe the promises he makes, it just somehow gets stuck in the zone of my brain that is reserved for 'knowledge' without transitioning to the point of accepting.

A book that has opened my eyes to new ways of thinking in this area is David Benner's *The Gift of Being Yourself: The sacred call to self-discovery*. One thing I enjoy about his writing is that he gets, and explores, this tension between objective knowledge of self and God and personal knowledge.

Essentially this is where I stumble. I am objective and logical in many ways. I can produce a masterful (well, not terrible) answer to many questions about faith, life and self-acceptance, but I struggle to believe that it is truly possible for me.

A friend of mine went on a retreat in order to try to work out his calling in life. He came away with the conclusion that he had no idea what his calling was, and the slight fear that he had 'wasted' the previous 15 years. But, he said, he was confident that this was not true and it was helpful to know that he wasn't sure of his calling even though he found it disconcerting. I launched into a mini preach about confidence, about the importance of trusting that God is in control, that he uses everything for good.

I used the example of a failed relationship of mine, which had been incredibly destructive for my emotional health; but through that experience I had met my husband. Even the things that feel like a waste of time, or are damaging, I said, can be used by God for good – that God loves us and lets us follow our passions. I essentially gave a detailed lecture about the importance of failure and acknowledging where we might have gone wrong.

When I came to do the editing of my book, I realized that this is all pure knowledge; I don't let it become something I trust and rely on, because really, it probably isn't safe. I can speak about it with others, but because there is so much in me that I don't like or trust, I cannot believe these things for me.

What Benner does is give me a language that adequately describes the way I am able to self-analyse. Objectively, I can see where I go wrong, I can trust that Mike, my friends and family do love me, and trust that God loves me *as I am*. I struggle to allow this self-knowledge to become personal understanding. To do this would mean accepting that I am not perfect, that it is OK for me to get things wrong, and learning to apologize when I do. This is where I always get stuck.

I am afraid that if I apologize to someone and ask for their forgiveness without justifying my bad (naughty) behaviour, they will respond by saying, 'About time!' or 'Well, so you should!' Then I will feel wretched and small (and they will be let off the hook for how they have behaved). As I already feel this way about myself, the outward confirmation would be crushing.

I struggle to accept that love is a real and permanent fixture in my life, regardless of how much I mess up, what I say or how I behave. I struggle to accept that the grace of God is enough to actually find me lovable. It comes down to security; if I can feel secure in the knowledge that God loves me, I don't need to fear rejection from those around me.

In 2 Corinthians 12.9 Paul says, 'but he said to me, "my grace is sufficient for you, my power is made perfect in weakness." Therefore I will boast all the more gladly about my weaknesses, so that Christ's power may rest on me.' This doesn't mean I should go all Rasputin and start doing bad stuff to see Christ at work! What it says is that my fear of failure, of being caught out in my bad behaviour, and hiding when I do, seeking to be seen as perfect – all this does not allow me to see Jesus work in my life. It is a way of hiding from grace, rejecting what he offered freely through his death.

I need to accept and trust in the love of family and friends; if I don't, I am essentially calling those I love liars. And truly accepting the love of God as a perfect love brings deeper knowledge and understanding that there is nothing I can do to sever or stop that love. Armed with this knowledge, I might just manage to be calm in the face of doubt. Trusting that when I fail I can take my failings to God, not be afraid of them, and receive his grace again, I might be able to respond rationally when I feel I am being told that I am in the wrong. The unconditional nature of the love of God brings security, but this is still something that I struggle to fathom or grasp.

I think it takes time to build up a recognition of self as someone worthy of love. So my resolution for now is to remember to think carefully before I react to an accusation. To pause, and consider the other person's perspective. To trust that, perhaps, the world won't end if they are right and I concede – just once, of course.

And finally, to be like Frank. To be confident in myself and humble in interacting with others. This, obviously, being very easy to do . . .

2 What sort of special?

My purpose in writing this book is to try to work out how to live a life in which I actually love myself as I am and for who I am. While most of us struggle with a certain amount of self-doubt and a lack of confidence, for some this is on such a significant scale that we are unable to accept and understand that we are, in fact, *worth* loving.

The Bible teaches us much about God's infinite love for us, but this rarely translates, for me, into actually believing it to be true. Society teaches us a more believable narrative – that we always need to be better than we are to be truly acceptable.

Films, adverts and magazines inform us that we need to be special, to stand out from the crowd, in order to be worth loving. We live in a culture where at least part of us believes that if we have recognition from certain people, we will feel better about ourselves.

Do you ever think that you would be happier if you were part of 'that' group? I have had this for most of my life. I identify a group of people – you know the type, funny, intelligent, good-looking and interesting; they have it all together and absolute confidence in themselves – and wish for recognition from them. I always figured that if those people acknowledged me, then I would be cool too. I would like myself more because I would believe that I was worth liking. It's a type of celebrity culture. There is a scale of celebrity – from the cool kids in school to the Angelina Jolies of the world – within each 'pond' people whose recognition is more significant and worth having than the rest.

I certainly crave this attention from the 'more important' people. And I feel endlessly guilty for wanting to be noticed. It seems obvious that it is counter-productive to seek my own advancement, to be elevated to a position above those around me – surely this will just lead to others feeling as I did before? Also, will it actually make me feel any better? Could I trust it? Is it believable as love?

The problem is, I want to be wanted. I want to be special. The Bible says that we are all uniquely special and valuable, which surely indicates that I am special. However, once I jump on to the following train of thought, I end up on a roundabout with no exits.

I want to be considered special; I want to be noticed; but we are all special, which leads to the question – what kind of special am I? And does the fact that I am special mean that I should be recognized above others as special? If we are all special, then how can I be actually special enough to stand out – should I even stand out? Maybe I should just be one of seven billion special people, but then see – I want to be recognized as special, as being of value.

So it goes on, until my head is spinning and my self-worth is plummeting, and I am convinced of my inherent arrogance in believing that I should ever be recognized over and above anyone else.

So, in a world that tells us we need to stand out to be valuable, combined with a faith that says we are all unique, but equally valuable: **what does it actually mean to be special?**

The Bible speaks of us being known before we were born (Jeremiah 1.5), being fearfully and wonderfully made (Psalm 139.14), known to the extent of the number of hairs on our head, and the most valuable of all God's creations (Matthew 10.29–31). Jesus was the great equalizer. Through his death, communication with God was opened up. Elevation above others is counter to the message Jesus brought, though Jesus' own disciples fell into this trap, and Christians ever since have not avoided the pitfalls of seeking to be seen as 'special' above others. Luke 9.46–48 shows the disciples wanting to be seen as greater than one another, and Jesus rebuking them, 'whoever is least amongst you will be greatest'.

Celebrity culture is a problem across society, and the Church has not been immune to those seeking a platform or position where they will be considered 'especially valuable'. Centre-stage roles have often become opportunities to be a 'celebrity'. Few seem able to resist the desire to be considered extra-valuable; and perhaps, in fact, we all want someone to elevate. It is not a deliberate thing, but one that we, as with wider society, have failed to avoid as we so often base our value on what others say of us.

My issue here is about exploring how to stand out in a way that honours and acknowledges those around me. I want to believe that I am special and worthy of note without this leaving me with the impression that I am better or more significant than others. I want to be satisfied with being the last, being genuinely humble, rather than faking it because that is the right thing to do – especially if I end up in a position of leadership where I could end up believing that I am deserving of extra attention and care.

I have believed the society lie, that to be valuable I have to be particularly special or significant, so I am afraid of not standing out as someone of extraordinary value. It's a complicated issue that causes me to divide myself into two parts. One gladly takes all the praise and value put on me, while the other is overwhelmed by shame for how selfish and arrogant I feel I have become.

Essentially, the desire to be 'known' for being something special and valuable is making it all about *my* insecurity and fear. I am so absorbed in what I am not, that I fail to acknowledge what it is that I am. The desire to be acknowledged as valuable surely comes down to my inability to acknowledge value in myself. **How do I find peace in my own inherent value in a way that isn't about being valued more highly than those around me?**

The Christian response is, whose glory is it anyway? At a Christian youth camp I went to as a teenager, one worship leader used to refuse to sign autographs, because autographs made his work about him, not about God. The idea of this has always stuck with me. I was so impressed with that ability not to get sucked into the praise and admiration – the point of what he was doing was to give glory to God. Where I might have a tendency towards false humility, he had true humility. He believed that the work he did wasn't about him.

I might be very good at saying that it is all for God, but the truth is that while I talk about God, and want to draw people to him, I also want some of the focus and attention for myself. My first concern after speaking is rarely whether people encountered God, but whether they tweeted about me (OK, so this is an exaggerated version of reality, but it illustrates my point!).

This is part of what my fear is based on. I am terrified that, out of my insecurity and need for affirmation, I will take the praise given and put it all on me, rather than remember that the gifts I have are God-given. It's not that I should not acknowledge my own talent, rather that my having that particular skill should not be used to elevate me above others.

The moment I accept a position that elevates me above those around me, I am susceptible to the fear of being ignored, or considered less worthy than others with more prominent roles. I can accept work that could elevate me so long as in doing so I don't accept the elevation.

It is all about the mindset. The child dying of starvation in a small rural village has to be considered of equal value and as immensely precious as the famous preacher or worship leader. Likewise, the person who attends church without volunteering is equally important to the community as the person who plays in the band. If we do not acknowledge this fact with humility and genuine passion we are likely to believe the hype that some people in our community are better than others. While that might make the few feel particularly special, it will certainly not acknowledge the God-given value in those around them.

A friend of mine serves regularly within the church community, helping out with children, leading a small group and offering an open welcome to anyone she encounters. However, she regularly found herself thinking that what she does is not all that important. It is not 'special', it's the boring stuff. She believes that those who preach or lead from the front are more worthy of attention and care than her. They are smarter and more holy.

We live in a culture that thinks that those who make the world go round – those who operate quietly in the background – don't need to be acknowledged in the same way as those who show up at the last minute and make a big show. We allow people to believe that they have less to offer, less to bring, than the few who are centre stage.

Without this particular friend and those like her who serve and care quietly with little reward or recognition, there would not be any children's work, small groups would not happen and there would be no sense of community for a big-name preacher to come and preach to. There would be no 'centre stage'; we each bring something valuable.

Yet, I find myself fooled into believing that because I some-times have an opportunity to speak from a stage, maybe what I do is worth acknowledging more than what she does. This can lead to the belief that some of us, by virtue of our gifts and opportunities, are inherently more important and valuable than others.

The Church is in a unique position to avoid this trap because we have the teaching that points to the fact that it is God's opinion of us that counts. Jesus stated plainly that 'the last will be first, and the first will be last' (Matthew 20.16), which should be grounds enough to avoid the trap of Christian celebrity, yet we all yearn to be loved, liked and praised. The Christian celebrity culture is growing in power, encouraging those not in positions of prominence to believe that their God-given gifts are somehow less valuable than those of the people who are offered the opportunity to use their gifts up front.

To bring this back to the issue at hand, the question 'what sort of special am I?' has as its basis the need to be something more because I don't believe that I am worth anything without validation from others. The answer is about recognizing that being special is not about what I do, it is what about I am; and everyone is special, simply because they are.

Separating out character and gifts is essential. If I seek to be valuable based on what I do, then my value will always be susceptible to being lost. I *will* fail in things, on a regular basis. However, if I base my value on who God has made me to be, then what I do is suddenly no longer about my accomplishment but about his glory. God's belief in my inherent value means that regardless of what happens in my life, I am special beyond description.

What I don't really know is how to turn this understanding into a practice of trusting in God's love for me above the affirmation offered by those around me. My confidence in myself and trust in God are easily and quickly overridden by a critical comment, or a word of praise for *me*.

I came across a beautiful passage by Marianne Williamson on the subject of 'our deepest fear', in her book *A Return to Love*. For me, this gives a new perspective on 'being special'. She talks about the importance of accepting our value, acknowledging our gifts and talents, but then using them to enable others rather than elevate ourselves (emphasis mine):

> Our deepest fear is not that we are inadequate. Our deepest fear is that we are powerful beyond measure. It is our light, not our darkness that most frightens us. We ask ourselves, 'Who am I to be brilliant, gorgeous, talented, fabulous?' Actually, who are you *not* to be? You are a child of God. Your playing small does not serve the world. There's nothing enlightened about shrinking so that other people won't feel insecure around you. We are all meant to shine, as children do. We were born to make manifest the glory of God that

> is within us. It's not just in some of us; it's in everyone. *And as we let our own light shine, we unconsciously give other people permission to do the same. As we're liberated from our own fear, our presence automatically liberates others.*

Marianne Williamson highlights perfectly the contrast between seeking renown for myself and seeking it for God. When we trust in God's value in us, and use the gifts he has given us, but do this with his glory in mind, we find that we liberate others into doing the same. This is in contrast to taking praise and the promotion of our value and using it to elevate ourselves in order to establish our value in our own minds and in those around us.

Essentially it is a matter of mind and heart. The mind tells us that we are of value only if others tell us so; the heart, when we trust in God, reminds us that we are of value no matter what others say or think. Where do we find our value? In what do we trust? This will be a lifelong struggle for me. I doubt my worth and right to be in any position of leadership; therefore when I am offered it with praise, I use it to lift myself up.

I want to know my value, though, my inherent 'specialness', and in a way that provides not just a little room but acres of space for others to do the same. Marianne Williamson encourages us to recognize our gifts and strengths while drawing us constantly back to God and into community. This is essentially the difference between a God culture and a celebrity culture.

Christian celebrity culture is fundamentally against God culture. It encourages the few to believe that they are valuable and the many to believe they are less so. While I know the words to use to make it clear that I don't believe I am among the valuable few, I fear that in my heart I give that toxic belief room to grow.

As I journey through the issues in this book I hope to come to accept that what I *am* is special, and what I *do* does not affect that in the eyes of God.

3 Affirmation

In this chapter I want to dig deeper into my need for the approval of others. The last chapter explored the damaging impact of this craving on how I view myself in comparison to others; now I want to explore the craving itself. Why is it that I depend so entirely on the opinion of others to find value in myself?

I have always needed this approval to find any sense of self-worth. I don't trust my own opinion of myself – previous attempts at this have led to self-loathing. While I am not my own number one fan, there are times when I do quite enjoy my life and see there is value in me. My friends and family seem to like me, and I am practising not rejecting their opinion of me. The conclusion I draw from this is that there must be some good in me.

This is a helpful acknowledgement to make that has led to a greater ability to recognize the good in myself, but it hasn't lessened my dependency on others' opinions of me.

My yearning for affirmation is paralysing. Writing this book has been a genuinely terrifying ordeal. What happens when someone says I am 'pointing out the obvious' or 'talking endlessly about herself, to no aid of anyone else'? What if they say I am just plain wrong?

I know it will happen. Criticism is a normal part of life. We all get things wrong, and say and do stupid things. Criticism isn't new either. Aristotle said that 'the only way to avoid criticism is to do nothing, say nothing, be nothing'. The thing is, though, I depend on other people telling me I am good, to know that I am good; if people tell me I am bad then I believe them without hesitation.

In Chapter 1, I mentioned my blog and the comment that maybe I should do a theology degree. This comment sent me into a spin. My assumption was not simply that the person disagreed with me, which he was at liberty to do, or that he was being a bit superior and patronizing, it was that I was a bad theologian, I was stupid and I should stick to talking about my emotions. I absorbed his negative affirmation as fact.

This is a habit that results in a constant fear of rejection. I don't believe that my family, friends, or anyone, will stick around unless I prove that I am worth sticking around for. If I appear to be anything other than exceptional, what possible reason is there for people to remain in my life? My desire to be seen as perfect means that when I fail, I get angry or miserable – which means that I spend a lot of my time like that, and that actually makes me meaner.

If you depend on outside affirmation to survive, it is never going to be quite enough. You always need more, a further confirmation of your abilities, in order to gain the hope of being 'enough'.

I have to admit that as I have got older I have become more content with my lot; I am happier to be me and less ashamed of my existence. This may have led me to develop a better baseline opinion of myself. It has certainly helped me to deal with the times when I am filled with shame for what I have said or done. However, I have a horrendous replay cycle in my head. Replay is a slightly warped rehash of an event, or how it has been received, played over and over.

Currently, I am replaying a conversation I had about a year ago. I was talking with a friend and I was being rude about some of his friends. I got on to my high horse and declared my opinion as fact while being totally insensitive to the feelings of those involved. I went on a bit about how his friends were nice but not nice people (you know, you think you are being diplomatic but you fail miserably because you are actually just being mean. Or is that just me? Hope not). I crossed a line, then apologized (taking responsibility – winning!) and we made up.

My replay, though, does not include any of the making up, nor my genuine apology and his acceptance. It doesn't include the more rational aspect of that discussion (in this case, dating in the Christian world; as this is the second story in this book where I have misbehaved, you see that it tends to get me fired up).

What is replayed is just the fact that I was rude about his friends, and as a result he will probably dislike me for ever. I am aware of an overwhelming sense of shame and a recurring list summing up my attributes:

- You are mean.
- You are unkind.
- You are horrible.
- You are useless.
- You are cruel.
- You are nasty.

This is one of my many replays. Replay is a subject I will devote more time to later in the book as it is such an issue for me. They are distorted and adjusted memories, which reinforce the fact that I am not worth much.

This underlies the desperate need I have for people to counteract my thoughts about myself. However, being told that I am kind is like applying a plaster to a gaping wound. I might not see the blood for a fraction of a second, but soon enough it will leak through. It is a temporary fix that does nothing to alter the fact that I am rarely a fan of myself.

The use of social media does little to help this desire to be told I am valuable, with its endless opportunities to be both valued and devalued. It offers immediate validation – an instant positive reaction to your post, perhaps – but when your 'joke' gets no response or your meaningful statement is ignored, it is very hard not to question how others see you. If no one indicates that what you have to say is of value, then surely that means it has no value, right?

Social media encourages comparisons. We are all selective in what we post, the filter we put on to our lives. This creates a perfect opportunity to judge ourselves against other people. Other people seem to live the perfect life, while we observe the reality of our boring day-to-day existence. I feel the need to seek affirmation from people who appear to have the ideal life. But we don't represent our whole lives on these platforms. Even those who talk about the darker side of life will often do it 'well'.

I first joined Facebook in 2006, when I was at university. My recollection is of people always updating their statuses (the days of Katharine Welby *is* . . .), which were usually 'happy', 'angry', 'tired', and posting photos. The photos were rarely polished, and often of very drunk people looking a bit of a mess.

Since then, people have become a lot more careful about what they put on there. It is now a way of showcasing our lives. We often use it to communicate with people we rarely see; we want to know how well others are doing and would like to be shown doing just as well. I have found that social media encourages me to need more affirmation not less (comparisons is another topic I will come back to later in the book).

I am aware that the solution is to actually trust that what we are is enough without needing it to be affirmed by every person we encounter. Before exploring this further, I ought to repeat that the purpose of this book is not about indulging my need to be told I am great. I am exploring how I might be able to trust that what I am is enough without needing to seek confirmation from others. Hopefully, others might find a way to do the same. This is not about self-pity but rather about confronting reality: a way of facing the genuine doubts we have about ourselves and exploring what success and failure look like in a less negatively biased light.

I am an external processor, which means that unless I speak things out loud I struggle to really understand my thoughts. I need the outside input. This is partly why I write – I put something on the page and have a revelation: 'Oh! So that's what I've been thinking!'

But this might be a huge contributor to my desire for external affirmation. It may partly explain why I get so stuck in negative cycles of thinking. It certainly ensures that the replay continues undeterred, until I have a chance to speak about it with someone.

I have recently been through a course of CBT (cognitive behavioural therapy), during which I found some tools that help me with this particular issue. The desire for affirmation comes from the firmly held belief that I am not good enough – as illustrated by the analogy above of putting a sticking plaster over a gaping wound. When I am complimented, instead of taking it as a lovely encouragement, I treat it as a cure for all my woes, only to be disappointed when I begin to doubt whether the compliment was really meant.

In CBT I discovered a useful way of analysing negative cycles of thinking. It is essentially a review, and it enables me, as an external processor, to check in with my thoughts before they start to spiral. While this model is based on all negative thoughts, I find it particularly helpful in combatting my need for affirmation. It comprises the following steps (based on those in Mary Burgess with Trudie Chalder, *Overcoming Chronic Fatigue: A self-help guide using CBT*).

1 Situation: what was I doing at the time the negative thought came about?
2 Emotion: How did I feel? (Rate the intensity 0–100%.)
3 Unhelpful thoughts: what thoughts went through my mind when I started to feel this way? (Rate belief 0–100%.)
4 Evidence for and against your thoughts: make a note of the evidence and note down potential errors in your thinking.
5 Alternative thoughts: write alternative thoughts that result from the balance of evidence in previous step. (Rate belief in each new thought 0–100%.)
6 Outcome: re-rate belief in original negative thought and the intensity of the emotion that accompanies it.

7   Action plan: what can I do now to combat that thought when it rises again?

My need for affirmation most often comes after an occasion that has caused me to have a replay, or after I have released a new blog or done a talk somewhere – something that has put me outside my comfort zone. When I was pregnant, I was so exhausted that I needed affirmation and praise for doing simple things like getting out of bed, or making a cup of tea for my husband. I needed him to say, 'Well done, you are brilliant,' to stem the tide of thoughts about how pathetic, weak and useless I am.

This CBT model means that when a thought occurs – 'That was the worst talk I have ever given', or 'I am so lazy, all I have done for Mike today is make a cup of tea' – that would usually make me seek out confirmation that my thinking is wrong, I try to think about it rationally myself.

I wouldn't say that this is a real fix; after checking in with my thoughts, I might still need confirmation that my new way of thinking is more accurate, but at least I am not stuck in such a negative place. If you struggle with this too, this way of analysing your thoughts might help you to adjust your thinking to a more realistic and hopefully positive line.

One thing this tool doesn't do is resort to the 'you are wonderful' position; the corrected thought may just be a less awful version of the original. If Mike has cooked dinner, walked the dog, cleaned the kitchen and cared for me (which was our daily reality during the pregnancy), and I have only managed to make him a cup of tea, then the alternative thought might not be, 'You are a wonderful housewife who is perfect'. More realistically, it might be, 'Mike does a lot for you, but he knows that you do all you can and he has chosen to love you in sickness and in health'. While it cannot take away all the pain of the negative thought, it corrects it to make it manageable.

The question now is how to take this one step further. Having worked out that negative cycles of thinking are wrong, what would it look like if we didn't have to re-evaluate our thinking all the time? What if we actually believed that there was value in us? It might be worth asking this question: **Why do I think I don't have value unless someone else tells me that I do?**

Is there something in your past, or the way you were spoken to by parents, friends or teachers, that has led you to believe that you don't have value? Or is it something you have learnt elsewhere?

I struggle to answer these questions – there is no event that particularly stands out, except perhaps the one I described in Chapter 1 where my friends decided to unfriend me (in an actual real-life way). This may have encouraged me to seek confirmation of people's 'like' of me, and led to the fear that they will suddenly disappear if I don't make myself likable enough. But I had been seeking affirmation long before then.

When I was growing up, as a family we moved house a lot because of my father's job. By the time I started secondary school I was on my fourth or fifth school. While I was good at assimilating quickly into any new environment, perhaps this was at the cost of something important. Perhaps in my yearning to be accepted I sacrificed what I am in order to be what I needed to be to fit in. In each new place I would adjust my accent, my music tastes, what I liked to do and the words I used, according to the situation so that I would be accepted.

I remember starting a new school when I was nine, at roughly the time the Spice Girls released their first single. One of my new friends asked me if I liked the song, and I said yes, although I had no idea what she was talking about, as I hadn't even heard of the Spice Girls. We then proceeded to sing it 'together' and do the dance – me about a second behind her all the way through. When I got home from school I told Mum I loved the Spice Girls and I needed the tape.

This could be one explanation for why I need others' affirmation to tell me I am acceptable. Although I don't adjust my character and tastes to fit in any more, there is still that yearning to be loved. I may have trained myself in childhood to believe that I was likable only if I could slot into the new school quickly; and I may have this residual belief that I need to be different from how I really am in order to be loved. This leads to my constant craving for affirmation, which will assure me that both the path I am on and what I do are acceptable to the people around me.

These are my own personal workings out of the above question, though they are probably only a part of the cause, and in need of further work. Exploring what has led me to this point has begun to help me understand the causes of this need.

I have identified a model that can help tackle negative thinking, and explored why I might think that way. However, as mentioned in the first chapter, it is the 'what' questions that really challenge me. So: **What would it take to believe that you are valuable without needing others to confirm it all the time?**

In attempting to answer this question, perhaps it would be helpful to look at whether our circumstances and experiences devalue us, and whether this is in our mind or the minds of others. For example:

- Circumstance – I live with three life-altering conditions: depression, anxiety and chronic fatigue syndrome. The last is improving bit by bit, but all three have a significant impact on what I can and can't do.
- Experience – I want to be able to participate more fully in life – I want to be reliable, but due to my health I have often cancelled things at the last minute. I feel I am observing life from the sidelines. I see my friends going out and leading busy lives and I want to do the same, but one or all of my health issues get in the way.
- Outcome – I feel that these things devalue me, and that I have to work extra hard to be accepted. The mental health problems do not help with my need for affirmation, because they tend to hear the negative responses over the positive. If I have twenty people saying I am good and one person saying I am bad, that is the one person I believe.

I don't think this is just my experience. It is harder to block out the negative voices when we don't trust in our intrinsic value to begin with. While it is true that circumstances can accentuate feelings that already make it hard to trust in our value, for me there is something deeper in how I view myself that needs to change.

So, back to the question at hand. To get biblical for a moment, Psalm 139 is particularly strong on this need for outside affirmation. We hear that God knew us from before we were born, and has known us every day of our lives. And he still thinks we are not only acceptable but precious.

Verse 14 in particular is a guide here: 'I praise you because I am fearfully and wonderfully made; your works are wonderful, I know that full well.' This is striking for me, because I struggle least to believe in God's existence when I look at creation: the beauty in the world, the diversity of creatures, flowers and landscapes. Nothing takes my breath away more than being up high on top of a mountain and looking out at nature. I believe that God created the world, and therefore I have to acknowledge that his works are wonderful. I do know that full well.

However, why do I find it so difficult to apply this to me? This is where verse 14 comes in so handy: I am fearfully and wonderfully made. If I believe that God's creation is wonderful, and that he took great care over it, then that leads me to the point where I have to accept that he took the same care over creating me.

This is not restricted to my physicality, but extends to my character too. He carefully created me, taking time to think through who I was and who I could be. But here, things could get complicated – does this mean that he created some people 'evil'? So to clarify, I think he knew who I *could* be if I chose to be. This has to give me strength and hope in the face of my self-doubt. My intrinsic value is in the fact that I am made in the image of God.

If we are dependent on what people think of us, there is no hope. Some people will like us, others won't; sometimes we will be likable but sometimes not. If we rely on what others think of us, we will be pulled in every direction: a chameleon changing colour depending on who we are with, losing sight of who we are at our core.

This is what I did at school. It is only in the last few years that I have begun to break that habit, and it is a scary journey, starting to search for the 'me' underneath the 'what I should be' that has been built up over the years.

At the end of the last chapter, I talked about the need to acknowledge who I *am* as the part of me that has the most value, rather than what I *do*. It is this journey of self-discovery that will help us most in accepting ourselves as valuable without the need for outside confirmation. For me, living as a reaction to others for so long led me to not really knowing who I am myself.

The truth is that if you continually strive to fit in, to be 'cool', to seek others' affirmation, the opposite will happen. You stop believing in or being able to receive affirmation. You start to believe that everyone is lying, because deep down you know that who they see is not really who you are. We need more and more affirmation to accept any of it.

So, I am going to accept that God knew me before I was born, that he knit me together in my mother's womb, that I am fearfully and wonderfully made. I might not feel it fully, but I commit to continuing to think about why I am seeking affirmation. Is it because I don't believe that I am valuable? Or is it just because it is nice to be encouraged?

Affirmation in itself is an essential part of life. We need the love and encouragement of others, but I want that affirmation to be no more than encouragement. I don't want it to be my lifeline any more.

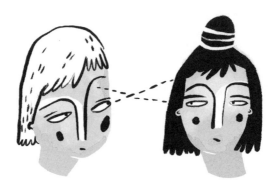

4 Comparisons

The issues I have explored so far all have a theme. Of course, a book needs a theme or it would just be a ramble, but the previous three chapters have all led to the obvious fact that I am more convinced of what I am *not*, and my failings, than what I *am*, can do, and my sense of self-worth. Chapter 1 focused on the fact that I don't take responsibility. Chapter 2 discussed my fear of becoming arrogant and of not being noticed. Chapter 3 explored my belief that I am not good enough and therefore need others to tell me who and what I am.

Now I want to think about the attributes that I do have. Through understanding what and who I am, I should be able to become more accepting of who and what I am not. Comparison seems, on the surface, to be focusing on the 'have not' aspect again, but bear with me.

Comparing ourselves to others is something I think we all do. It is very hard not to – we look at someone we admire and wish that we had what they have. This feeds pretty drastically into my need for affirmation, I think, and certainly encourages me to ask the question, what sort of special am I? I find it difficult not to compare my life with those of people around me. I either want to be like them, or alternatively feel slightly superior because my life seems to be going better than theirs.

I don't tend to compare myself so much to my friends, and I sometimes wonder whether this is the reason I am friends with them. Do I befriend people whose lives feel safe, and so they are unlikely to cause me to be jealous of them? I know my answer to this is no. My friends are some of the most inspiring people I know – people who have faced enormous challenges and accomplish great things.

The reason I don't compare myself to them is because I know them so well. I know the reality of life for them, and the struggles they face. The people I compare myself to are those I hardly know – people I've just met or follow on Instagram, or friends I don't see very often and are not close to. These people seem to have it all together: they look constantly cool, or they cook wonderfully, they go on adventures all over the world, have great talents and gifts, and honestly seem to live a perfect life.

The reality is that many of us will look like that to someone who doesn't know us well. It is easy to imagine that someone's life is perfect and more exciting than our own when we can't see behind closed doors. Social media can exacerbate this – although, of course, the problem of comparisons existed long before the advent of social media. We see people's global travels, beautiful clothes, cute children, and we may think that they must have life sewn up. We don't often see pictures of kids driving their parents up the wall, or a couple having a blazing argument, or the mess the kitchen is in after they've been cooking.

I have a habit of sharing my emotional mess with the world, but recently, since I had my son, my social media posting could paint a picture of a happy, rosy life. There are many photos of him, with a bit of Mike and a bit of Monty (our fluffy, teddy-like dog) thrown in for good measure.

I don't write much about the stress of parenting. While I'm always thinking of potential subjects for a blog, I often just don't have the time or energy, and on really bad days I don't tend to feel like posting anything. Why invite loads of people into our pain? I'd rather speak to my husband, my mum or a couple of friends at most.

The other day I was really struggling, but managed to write and post a blog during nap time. That helped me, but it was a polished version of the reality – edited and tidied; a complete stranger would not pick up on the real ups and downs of my daily life.

But then, most people are better behaved in public than at home, and we talk more about our triumphs than our failures. I don't blame anyone for that – sharing the messiness of my life with a complete stranger is not always what I feel like doing (says the woman writing this book, but it's different in person . . .). We change our behaviour depending on who we are with, and we feel safer with some people than with others.

The danger comes when we consciously develop an image that is not a true reflection of what life really is.

This isn't exclusive to social media, of course. I think most of us will dress up a bit, make an effort, when we are going to see people or having friends over. I am pretty certain no one is interested in seeing photos of the routine of my life, or hanging out with me when I haven't bothered to shower or brush my teeth.

However, we should consider carefully why we put effort into certain things and the picture it presents. Are we trying to keep up with the Joneses, or do we want to avoid boring the world with our TV habits? Social media can be the enemy of anyone who cannot help but compare their life to that of those around them – or that has been how I have felt anyway.

One danger with comparisons is that it is easy to see that there is always someone who possesses a gift you don't. I am not brilliant at organization, for instance. In fact, that is a complete understatement – I just throw stuff out into the world and hope it comes together well.

When it comes to organizing things I get stressed. The perfect example of this was our wedding, which was the most stressful thing I have ever done, although I did enjoy the day. But certainly wouldn't want to go again! We didn't do any sensible things like list-making until we were a few months in. I remembered to sort out the flowers only three weeks before the wedding. There were many compliments about how beautifully colour coordinated the wedding was, but that was a complete accident. I just wanted a wedding with a lot of colours in it. I didn't plan for my shoes to match Mike's kilt, I just thought the shoes were pretty! It was very colour coordinated, but that was just a lucky coincidence. My organizational attempts don't always come out looking so good.

I am likely to compare myself to, and be jealous of, those whose lives appear to be very organized, neat and tidy, and also those who are adventurous. I wish I was adventurous, but I confess, I am a home girl! I like to go on holiday, but I enjoy coming back home just as much. I like to know what to expect when I am away, so a holiday where we wouldn't know where we were staying from week to week would be a nightmare. I wish I had the sort of adventurous spirit that some of my friends have, where they experience the world in all its diversity, but when I try to be adventurous I can't help but wonder if I am doing it right. Surely it's not meant to be so stressful?

Illness enhances my comparison game. Being forced by illness to spend so much time at home means that I can't help but wish I was half as capable as others. At the height of my pregnancy I was pretty much housebound, and I found then that comparisons were often not about significant things, like holidays or fancy clothes. They concerned quite minor things, like the ability to do a full-time job or go for a walk in the sun, but these things convinced me that my life was not favourably comparable in any way to the lives of those around me.

Comparisons for me are as much about what I am not good at, or can't do, as the achievements of others. While the presenting of a perfect happy world gets my little insecure lights flashing, it is also the realization that I will never be the kind of person who can do tons in one day, or who likes to travel the world.

My latest comparison game concerns baby development. Many new mums seem to fall into this trap, and I am alarmingly aware of being a cliché. The other day I was with a mum whose little girl is a week younger than my son, Elijah, and she could sit SO much better than he could. I was amazed, and my friend said that she practises a lot. When I got home I promptly started sitting Elijah up on the bed. Again and again. Fortunately he thinks it is hilarious to fall over on to the soft mattress, and after several attempts we both were in fits of giggles. Honestly, I am fairly sure he will sit solo in his own good time, and fortunately falling over is funny.

I am not comfortable or at home in my own skin; I cannot acknowledge much that is good in me. Therefore, I figure being someone else, or having their skill-set, must be better than being myself. But then, in being someone else I would look around and see another person who it is an awful lot better to be. The insecurities of motherhood have certainly enhanced this trait in me.

If I spend my life comparing myself to others, though, then I cannot ever really be truly present in myself. I spend so much of my time wishing I was more like them and very little time actually considering what it means to be me.

Another problem is that I can find this comparison game easier than being me. The reality of life as 'me' is sometimes a little too much to handle. It is simpler to look at what I wish I was and strive to accomplish that (even if it is never going to happen) than actually consider what I am.

As with most of the issues I face concerning recognizing the unique value in being me, avoidance is key to successfully not dealing with them. Comparison offers a distracting path off the road of self-discovery. It enables me to spend any amount of time maintaining the belief that I have no value when put next to others. It provides a reason why others might think me worth less than them, which feeds my understanding that I am not good enough.

Without comparisons, I would have to look at myself, which means recognizing both faults and talents in equal measure. I am not good, though, at giving them equal space.

I realized a while ago that I never expect anyone to remember my name. I was at an event recently and bumped into someone I had met a few years earlier. She had made a big impact on me and I was excited to talk to her again, so I introduced myself to her (again), only to be stunned that she already knew who I was. Not only did she remember me, she seemed surprised that I would remember her.

This was new to me. I had spent a few years in a large church, where I would meet someone one week, then when I saw them again the next they would not remember me and would introduce themselves again. The thing is, I never thought it odd that people couldn't remember me; I thought it was perfectly reasonable. I might get a little irritated if the same person did it three or four weeks running, but, honestly, I would entirely understand.

There was one week I went to church and bumped into the vicar. He had known my dad for decades and I had spoken to him the week before. However, I opened with: 'Hello! Do you know who I am?' I admit, the way I phrased it was a little weird. I was just trying to be helpful and avoid that awkward 'the vicar is trying to remember my name without showing that he has forgotten it' thing, which I had seen my dad do countless times. He had remembered me, of course; but I felt that next to so many other people, I would be utterly forgettable.

Since I have been speaking up about my mental health problems, though, and the fact that half my surname is relatively recognizable in some Christian circles, a side effect has been that increasingly people remember me. I may not be so easily forgotten, but this has had no impact on my comparison game.

I used to see 'cool' people who are recognizable and I would understand why they are remembered. Even though people remember my name now more often than before, I can't help wondering, if my dad wasn't 'important' and fond of funny hats, would I be remembered at all? Because my assumption is that others largely think similarly to me, that must mean that they have a very low opinion of me. I live in their minds, form their opinions for them, and establish that really I do not compare. I long to be more like them, so that I will be worthy of their time and attention.

All this brings me to the question I want to ask here, which is: **Is your view of yourself/my view of myself realistic or not?** This is one to ponder, especially if you struggle significantly with comparisons.

If you can recognize that you see yourself in a more negative light than those around you perhaps do, and that there may be more to you than meets your inner, overly critical eye, even if it's in just one area of your life, then progress is being made. This requires self-awareness, which requires us to know a bit about our strengths. Is it realistic for you to compare yourself to certain people? If your own strengths lie elsewhere, no amount of striving will lead you to a life like theirs.

I am gradually coming to recognize that I have more value than I give myself credit for. I find myself able to stand among those whose lives I wish mine resembled; I feel that I am not quite such a loser, and I am relatively certain that I have skills that are desirable to others. This is progress, even if it is slow.

The Bible is pretty clear on this. God stated it to Moses, in the Ten Commandments: 'You shall not covet . . . your neighbour's ass' (Exodus 20.17, AV). The teenager in me always has a giggle at this one. I am fairly sure that I often covet others' asses in the modern sense (a fitter, healthier body, in other words). Frivolity aside, the Bible is full of our unique value to God. Psalm 139, which I explored in the previous chapter, is just one of the many examples.

Jesus died for me – individually, as well as for the collective world. He sees a value in me that is precious. He knows me down to the number of hairs on my head (Luke 12.7), he knew me before the world began (Ephesians 1.4), and he knitted me together in my mother's womb (Psalm 139.13). That amount of care and attention to detail should give me fundamental proof that I don't need to compare myself to those around me, and that I am, in fact, exactly who I was meant to be.

One of my favourite verses is Esther 4.14: 'And who knows but that you have come into your royal position for such a time as this?' Such a powerful thought and one that echoes far beyond Esther. Women at the time of this story were pawns in the games directed by men. Esther had no choice about whether or not to marry the king. The idea offered in this verse, though, is that we are all born to be who we are, when we are.

Comparing myself to others denies the possibility that what I am is, in fact, exactly what is needed now, for such a time as this. I may not become royalty and save my entire race from extinction, but I might have some value to add to the world. Even so, when I observe a fault in myself I do wonder why God allowed such a mistake to pass. This is perhaps one illustration of my struggle to trust in God. It seems easier to trust the more obvious opinion of my own thoughts and what I believe others think of me.

I want to find faith in God's opinion of me. I want to believe that I am incomparable to others, because I am uniquely and carefully made – in the same way others are incomparable to me. The decision to accept my God-given value made at the end of the last chapter applies here too; more than that, here there is the need to establish an acceptance in me of my inherent value. While an understanding of the fact that God puts value in me is essential, it is important for me to identify and explore that value. What is it in me that makes me valuable?

This is where this chapter ties in with the previous two. The need for affirmation is not helped by constant comparisons to others, and this is very similar in theme to the 'what sort of special am I' question. All three feed into one another; it is hard to determine which comes first.

As far as I see it, I compare myself to others and this leads to the need for affirmation to establish that I am as good as they are; this in turn leads to the risk of accepting praise and position that elevates me above others, in order to feel that I do actually compare favourably. It is a cycle in which none of the issues at hand really helps to manage any of the others.

So, a final question to ponder: **What would it take to stop you feeling the need to compare yourself to those around you?**

My first answer when I asked this of myself was, 'Well, I need to be more organized, more outgoing, more ambitious and better.' This is not very useful, or honest, and is reliant on me changing; it also negates the entire point of the book, which is to explore the idea that what I am, now, is good.

Thinking more deeply about the question, it comes down to accepting who you are for what you are (sorry about the cliché) – ever so simple to say, very hard to do; in fact, a monumental task for anyone struggling with their own self-worth.

A simple starting point might be to try to list the things that I am. If I can respond to my constant thinking of what I am not, compared to others, perhaps I can point out what I am as I am. This is something I resist, though. My great fear is that in doing so I will become arrogant, and gain an inflated sense of my own value. Whenever I think something positive about myself I tend to almost punish myself. Others may tell me I am good, but I can't tell myself! In my mind it is like jumping on a slide leading into a pit of arrogance and pride.

This ensures that I remain trapped in a place of low self-esteem, in a constant vicious cycle: compare, be affirmed, get praise, let it go to my head, realize I am horrible, then back to the beginning.

The comparisons game is all about looking at what others have that you lack. It rarely sees what is below the surface or acknowledges life's complications. It is purely about seeing a better option – the grass is always greener. I really don't know how to counter this, other than looking more closely at what I have, and what I wish I had.

Take the example of those with an adventurous spirit. I could look at friends' holiday pictures and feel envy, or I could acknowledge that it looks great fun . . . for them. The truth is, I wouldn't really enjoy their adventure-filled trips. I like my home comforts, and love quietly reading in the sun in a peaceful place. I could think how boring I am, next to them, or I could acknowledge that what is great for them would not be great for me.

This is something I have been working on over the past year. Every now and then I get a twinge of envy, but it is more usual for me to be able to look at photos of other people's grand adventures and enjoy them for what they are – pretty pictures of other people's adventures. Nowadays I rarely find the need for comparison regarding this particular hang-up, because I have accepted that I am not adventurous.

This 'looking at what I am' method is interesting; so far, it has only been a success on the holidays and adventures thing. Other comparisons that are very prevalent are harder to tackle; things like organization, parenting and cooking/fitness. Some of these (for example, parenting) stem from insecurity; the others come from not accepting that my version of what I do is as good as what I compare it to.

I am increasingly willing to acknowledge that I am not as good as other people at many things; but that doesn't mean I cannot do anything, nor that others are better than me at everything in life. It is about accepting that we are all different. Others may be brilliant at things that I am only OK at, but there are things that I excel at that others perhaps struggle with. This growing realization has made me happier to share in the lives of those I encounter, without coming away feeling smaller. I have value; I am good at things.

These two simple acknowledgements have made a huge difference to the way I compare myself to others and where I am willing to look for my value.

The idea that I could have been made, designed and created, with specific gifts and character unique to me, like Esther 'for such a time as this', is a powerful incentive to find value in myself. If I believe that God made me, and trust that he has known me from before I was born and took great care in creating me, then it must follow that there is a reason I am me – and not whoever I happen to be comparing myself to today.

5 The inner conflict

So far in this book all the subjects I have talked about are related and encourage one another. The issue of inner conflict is no different. When I explained to my counsellor what I wanted this chapter to say, she pointed out that what I was describing was in fact perfectionism.

Comparisons, the need for affirmation, the inability to take responsibility and the 'what sort of special' question are all insecurities that feed into the need to *present* a perfect image of myself to the world. This goes beyond the image I want to present; getting things wrong or failing requires me to consider who I am. I want to *be* perfect. I don't want to face my own inability and imperfection myself, let alone have anyone else see it.

This chapter is in effect the story of me vs me. The 'what sort of special' subject, explored in Chapter 2, is really the externalization of an inner debate. That chapter explored the added complications of celebrity culture and socially helpful behaviour (how you behave towards others amid your own insecurities); here this issue is focused on a realistic understanding of self. A realistic understanding of self may help in tackling the need to be considered special by others.

I have often thought that, really, I am two people. There are huge conflicts inside me, although as I have got older some of these conflicts have resolved themselves and I am less likely to have two opinions on the same subject, which has often been a symptom of this issue. However, motherhood is bringing the issue of two conflicting opinions to the surface again.

For example, me with a one-week-old: 'I would never cover my baby's head when he is feeding; people who are uncomfortable can just deal with it.' Me with a two-month-old: 'I have to cover his head when he is feeding; he is impossible to feed in public and I am tired of flashing my breasts at the whole church.' Both these thoughts still remain in my head. I object but I also am totally on board. It's impossible.

Essentially, I have two voices inside me, one that says, 'You are nothing, a failure and a fraud and will never amount to anything,' and one that says, 'You will win an Oscar!' despite the fact I have never acted in my life and have no desire to start.

I don't know how to get the balance right between the two. On my confident days, the sky is the limit and I could do anything. The problem then is that in my head I start imagining myself doing things that won't happen, because they are so unrealistic. The counter-balance is the not believing I can do anything, which is equally unrealistic.

I want to be able to find the right balance between these two opposing beliefs – where I know that I have skills and capacity to do what I am good at, but also where my expectations are realistic.

This doesn't mean not dreaming; I want to have my ambitions met, to accomplish things to the extent of my capacity. I don't want to be mediocre; I want to excel at what I do. However, in the day-to-day thinking process, I need to find a way to dream these dreams while keeping them realistic, and not get carried away into a fantasy land where I am a master of martial arts, who saved the world with ridiculously fabulous exposé articles on something very important. The problem is, the bigger my dreams get, the more I find myself believing in my own supreme inadequacy. Whenever I find myself in a position of success, I question my right to be there. I am certain that there are people (and plenty of them) who are equally if not more deserving of the position I find myself in.

I seem to be incapable of finding a place where my expectations are enough to challenge me to do my best without expanding that into the faraway realm of fantasy. That fantasy comes from a place of insecurity (who is shocked?). I doubt my worth, so I find a way of being worthwhile that is all in my head. I am then stuck in a place where what I consider to be worthwhile is not achievable for me (or, to be honest, for anyone), and that can leave me with only one conclusion. I am not worthy.

I want to be ambitious in a way that is realistic to achieve. I want to be satisfied with my success and content with the path I am on. This is where the damage of comparisons plays its part. I am constantly looking at others, comparing their successes and ambitions with mine (often seemingly small and insignificant), and that does not help me to accept that my skill-set is enough. But often I do not consider the stage of life these people are at, or the field they work in. A successful lawyer might have taken years to climb the ranks. What would similar or equal success look like in my field? How is it even comparable? And if that lawyer is five years older than me, why should I be at the same point in life as them anyway?

The truth is that I don't really trust that what I am is enough to accomplish anything. I wish I was braver, bolder, and better in what I do. My accomplishments create an imposter syndrome in me – the undeserved recognition of achieving what hundreds of people could have done better. The things I fail in only confirm my belief that what I am is never going to be enough.

The negative programming of my brain, together with the constant comparisons that society encourages us to make, leads me to the conclusion that the only way to achieve anything is within the fantasy of my mind. But this internal life neither enables me to do anything nor aids me in my dreams.

The unrealistic leaning towards both my potential successes and my obvious failings produces a paralysis, as if I am stuck in a bog. My feelings of inadequacy and a fear of failing mean that often I don't do anything. Finding a point of balance between realistic thinking and expectations would, I hope, enable me to accomplish things that I could be proud of without feeling that any success is undeserved. I have no idea, as yet, how to even begin trying to find that balance, though. It seems an impossibility, because of the voice in my head that says, 'Really, let's face it, I know what I am and I am not enough.'

If I could reprogramme my mind, that might be the place to start! I wish I could do something like Chuck (a TV show character, for those wondering who I am talking about). Chuck has a super computer in his head. It was accidentally downloaded into his brain and he can 'flash' on random things. He helps the CIA catch criminals and bring them to justice.

Chuck, understandably, doesn't particularly like having this super computer in his head and he wants it out. To cut a long story short, he discovers that he needs to 'overwrite' his brain, essentially resetting his mind back to before having the super computer. There is more to the story, of course, but my point is that this action takes just a few minutes. I would like to be able to overwrite my brain, to find a better, happier way of thinking. It would be great to hit a button and a few minutes later be able to think in a new way about myself, my value and worth, my skills – the lot.

As I said at the beginning of this chapter, my counsellor suggested that I appeared to be talking about perfectionism. On that subject, a book I have found useful is *The Perfectionism Book* by Will van der Hart and Rob Waller. It is well worth reading, if you struggle with this too, and to work through the exercises it contains.

In the conversation with my counsellor I was a bit thrown, as I have spent much of my adult life determinedly avoiding thinking about my perfectionism. I have always justified this by saying, 'I can't be a real perfectionist because I can never finish anything,' or 'because I honestly don't have the drive to do everything well.'

I am not a 'super successful' perfectionist, someone who excels at everything but still thinks they are not good enough. I am instead excessively hard on myself, because I can never accomplish what I think I should, so I back away from trying to avoid that awful crush that failure brings.

One element of perfectionism that van der Hart and Waller talk about is the impact it has on our self-esteem. This is what I really want to explore in this chapter – the fact that I largely base my self-esteem on whether I have achieved the goals I set for myself.

I have found in recent years that I am increasingly able to set more realistic goals in life. Take this book. It is something that

I can actually do (unlike winning an Oscar). The problem is, my fantasy world takes over this attainable goal and turns it into a fanciful story: this book will sell thousands of copies, then I will write another that will sell even better, and then I will get into fiction writing and become the next J. K. Rowling; and then obviously my Twitter game will rise to meet her incredibly high standard.

The realistic goals I set become overwhelmed with the unrealistic. Then, when I achieve the realistic goals, I am still convinced of my failure because I can't possibly keep up with the unrealistic goals – and the realistic goals have become less interesting and appealing by comparison. This book is unlikely to sell thousands of copies, and I am unlikely to become a bestselling novelist – not least because I don't write very good fiction, and I don't have the will to try.

However, I get so absorbed in what 'should' be the natural progression of book-writing success that I fail to take account of the fact that I have actually got halfway through writing a book. I am actually close to achieving what I set out to achieve. It may not be the best book in the world, and it may get a few negative responses, but this is something that before seemed insurmountable. I want to be able to enjoy this success, not be fixated on what 'should' come next, or indeed how much better this book could be.

All my thoughts and fears – worry about how others see me, comparisons to those around me, a constant need for affirmation and confirmation, and inability to take responsibility – are fed by this perfectionist mentality.

I am writing this book, but I don't want to have to think about whether it is any good, or listen to what people think of it, and I don't want to face the rejection that will inevitably follow. I am embarrassed and ashamed sitting here writing this. How will people take it? What will they say? Will it be good enough? Or is it too 'me centric' and therefore of no use to anyone but myself? Who will leave the first negative review? What if no one reads it?

These thoughts go round and round, but the truth is that unrealistic ambitions are what keep me moving forward. They prevent me from having to think realistically, about how others will react, because in my fantasy the book has been universally well received.

Brené Brown tackles this beautifully in *The Gifts of Imperfection*, which could be another book for your 'to read' pile: 'Perfectionism is a self-destructive and addictive belief system that fuels this primary thought: if I look perfect and do everything perfectly, I can avoid or minimize the painful feelings of shame, judgment, and blame.'

While the way I operate within my perfectionism is different from this, the purpose is the same. I avoid doing things because I am aware of my inability to do them to a perfect standard, and I don't want the feelings of shame, judgement and blame. When I do step out, such as with this book, these feelings come to the fore. I know I will not write the perfect book, so in order to avoid those feelings I fantasize; I would not write a word otherwise.

So, to summarize, I acknowledge that I need to deal with my perfectionism and I recognize the power it has over my life and activities. Now I want to actually learn how to put it down!

Essentially, I am afraid to consider what realistic success might look like. I worry that if I examine my goals and expectations, I will prove myself to have fallen short of what I think I *should* achieve in life. This has a huge impact on my self-esteem and on my ability to accomplish anything.

The root appears to be in what I believe I *should* accomplish. I remember a discussion I had with a friend some time ago about how the 'should' of life drives us. We have both had severe depression, which has had an impact on our work, including periods of serious illness during which we have been unable to work at all. He mentioned that when he was really ill, someone said to him, 'Don't should on yourself.' My friend made this quite an amusing anecdote, as the guy who had said it to him had a strong accent, so it sounded a lot like 'Don't s**t on yourself' – also sound advice, although it really wasn't an issue for my friend, even at the peak of his depression.

I found this incredibly simple but helpful advice. It is somehow both blindingly obvious yet so easy to miss. And I have made progress in reducing the exceptionally high expectations I have for myself in areas such as social situations and managing my health, but I still have a lot to do when it comes to expectations regarding work and relationships.

My hope is that by tackling this root of high expectation, I will be able to lessen the fantasy response that keeps me in the cycle of never achieving what I think I should. I have been using *The Perfectionism Book* in looking at how I can do this, and one thing the authors talk about is rules vs guidelines. This is essentially the basis on which we determine what we *should* be doing.

They suggest an exercise where you list the 'rules' you have for yourself and then try to turn them into 'guidelines'. The two can be very similar. The difference is in the emphasis and the stress that the rules put you under. An example of this, for me, would be as follows:

Rule	**Guideline**
I must post a blog every week.	I will aim to post a blog each week.

'Aiming' to post a new blog each week allows flexibility. If I have been very busy and not inspired to write anything new, then I don't need to feel under pressure to accomplish something that could wait until I have a bit of spare time.

With this example, of course, I started writing a blog because it helped me to process what was happening in my head. If I focus on the rule – I *must* – then writing it becomes less about its original function and more about pressure, expectation, perfectionism and performance.

In reality, even my guideline here is unrealistic. A better guideline might be to aim for one blog a month. If I do more, yay! But if I don't, once a month is a success. Looking at my posting record over the past year, once a month is more than my average recently, but it feels achievable. Once a week is a guideline I think I *should* be achieving, which defeats the whole point of the exercise.

So experience suggests to me that it is worth setting guidelines and then revisiting them later to assess whether you have in fact given yourself a rule under the guise of a guideline. The exercise has turned out to be very helpful for me, not least in increasing my awareness of the extent of my unrealistic expectations.

On a larger scale this can be applied to the book. When I was writing this chapter originally, what was driving me was that I *must* finish the book before the end of August. I was still writing it the following April. There was little flexibility within my mind, which meant that I experienced an enormous amount of pressure; this caused me to get nervous and back away from writing at all. Better to fail because I haven't tried than to fail because what I did was simply rubbish.

Putting a guideline in place would have taken the pressure off. For example, 'I *want* to finish the book by the end of August, but I am pregnant and my baby is due in September, so if it all gets too much I will put it down and come back to it later.' Instead, I kept piling the pressure on until I hit breaking point; my mental health was deteriorating and it was having a negative effect on my pregnancy.

Failing to finish the book before I gave birth actually turned out to be a very good thing. Coming back to writing it months later, with fresh eyes and ideas and a slightly different view of the world, has been incredibly helpful. If I had finished it when first planned, I would be releasing a book that I was extremely dissatisfied with – a book about 'loving yourself' that would have caused me to really not 'love myself' at all.

The rules vs guidelines exercise has helped me to examine the way in which I operate, though it seems that I have a way to go before being able to set realistic guidelines. The examples I have used illustrate, on reflection, how much I expect of myself. If used properly, the flexibility in the guideline enables me to be realistic about what is achievable, which in turn helps me not to head into the world of fantasy and give up on reality.

Essentially, flexibility enables me to work rather than procrastinate.

6 Your crap, my crap

Boundaries is a huge topic – good and bad boundaries, how to make them, maintain them and ensure they are healthy for you and those around you. I have read many books on the subject containing some very clever and amazing theories.

Dr Henry Cloud is an author I particularly like on this topic; while his *Boundaries* is great, my favourite book is *Changes That Heal*. I read what he writes and I think, yeah! I want that – all that healthy stuff in my life. I want boundaries both to protect myself and to help me love others. Then I try and enact the theory, someone pushes the limit and I react either by exploding – red face, loud voice, shaking hands sort of rage – or quietly submitting.

As I have got older, I have become more confident with the idea that people shouldn't push my boundaries, and I'm likely to react when they do. These days, though, it is not so much people's actions that are invasive but their emotional issues; it is my emotional boundaries that are low. You may know the feeling: a friend tells you that they are really struggling with something in their life and it becomes the only thing you can think about.

I get that all the time – but not as in 'look at me, so loving and caring that all I do is worry about my friends', more in an 'oops, I forgot that I am not them' sort of way. I become so emotionally involved that I forget that actually I can't fix their problems, and they aren't even mine to fix. This prevents me from being able to support them; I stop being objective and there for them, and start to get depressed by the extra emotional baggage I seem to be carrying.

A few years ago I had several friends who were experiencing various problems, including relationships and singleness, bullying by people who should have known better, illness, infertility, and work. It was a very stressful time, though not for the reasons you might expect. I was battling depression and anxiety, about to get married, was trying to adjust to my dad suddenly being in the news A LOT, along with various other dramas, but all this was not what was keeping me up at night – it was my friends' troubles. I was so wrapped up in what they were dealing with that I was failing to consider my own emotional and mental well-being, to invest enough in my relationship with Mike, or to prepare myself for the changes happening in my life.

This came out in two ways. The first was when Mike and I had spent some evenings watching episodes of *Game of Thrones* and *House of Cards* together. I found that afterwards I was going home from his flat feeling miserable, and I couldn't work out why. Both shows contain some pretty depressing elements, but they were getting into my head. Like really into my head. The end of *Game of Thrones* season one, for example, caused me to spend days saying, 'I can't believe that happened! Why would they do that?' It was making me miserable.

This should have been a warning sign that I was taking on other people's crap rather more than was healthy, and so I was not giving my crap the time it deserved. But I didn't get the warning.

The second incident was when I realized how much 'thought time' I was giving my own life compared to how much I gave everyone else. At the time of my wedding, I was so wrapped up in a haze of issues concerning those around me that I hadn't considered fully the impact of getting married, to the level it deserved, on myself and my life. The result was me calling my mum the day after the wedding, in the midst of an anxiety attack, and her very calmly saying, 'You did want this, you know you did! Think about it for a minute,' with Mike standing next to me rubbing my shoulders with a slightly anxious look on his face. I did want it; it was exactly what I wanted. He was exactly what I wanted.

Now don't get me wrong, I fully believe that we should care about, love and support our friends. We should be there for them. The problem comes when our 'being there' becomes feeling sad for them and so overwhelmed by the sheer weight of their issues that we cannot support them or ourselves.

We need to ask the question, whose crap should we carry? If I try to carry yours as well as my own, I get squashed by the weight of it. And in my case this leads to a mushy mind and a whole world of brain malfunction.

Distinguishing between what is my issue, such as 'I need a job', and what is a friend's issue – 'she needs a job' – is crucial. I can pray for my friend, walk alongside her, encourage and listen to her, but I can't apply for the jobs for her. If it's me looking for a job, I actually have to work out what I want to do and why. If I spend all my time worrying about my friend, that doesn't help her, and it doesn't help me either.

There are, however, helpful things I could do in this example. I could research jobs with her, and help review applications – as long as I know exactly what she is looking for and I'm not adding to her stress levels. But I am so busy worrying about everything for her, I don't actually think of these helpful types of things until too late.

The irony is that while I struggle to take responsibility for my own stuff, I am more than willing to make excuses for others, and attempt to fix any issue they might have, regardless of whether I have the skills required or the capacity to do so. Also – I HATE it when people try to solve my problems for me, but still have the desire to fix everyone else's. Really, I just have it all backwards.

I feel that I am afraid of taking the time to look at my life, to consider and deal with my issues, so instead I hide behind the pretence of helping others. At the same time I get increasingly stressed, overwhelmed and tired. It's emotional procrastination.

Caring for people is a healthy, human response and an important community-focused thing to do. Biblically we are called to recognize and feel one another's pain: Romans 12.15 says, 'Rejoice with those who rejoice; mourn with those who mourn.' In order to show our love for those in our community, we need to acknowledge their hurt and pain as well as their joy and successes.

However, to go alongside this healthy care for those I love, I need to recognize what it is that I gain from this particular problem. This in turn may help to lead me to a place of caring for others in a way that is helpful for both them and me.

My counsellor is a big advocate of the idea that we gain something from everything we do (whether positive or negative). One reason we may regularly do the same wrong thing is because we gain something from it. Jealousy is the only exception: it just hurts both us and the person we are jealous of (if they are aware of it).

For example, let's go back to Chapter 1 and my refusal to take responsibility for my actions. If I point out the faults of the other person who I think has provoked my bad behaviour, then I am spared the weight of being the only one in the wrong. Rather than saying sorry and having a calm conversation, I lose my temper and accuse them of wrongdoing, which has led me to behave badly. It lets me off the hook.

If this is an issue for you, take a moment to consider this. **What is it that you get from focusing on your friends' problems at the expense of your own?**

For me, it is fairly obvious. In a similar way to comparing myself to others, as discussed in Chapter 4, it is a distraction. If I look at others, I don't have to look at me. Because I don't like myself terribly much and am horribly aware of my failings, it is a relief to take the opportunity to concentrate on someone else, which makes me feel useful and valuable.

This need to be distracted from myself is apparently extremely common, or so I've been told. However, being aware that I resort to using my friends' problems to distract me from my own issues tends to fill me with guilt, shame and negative feelings, partly because I feel that after a decade of counselling I should have some idea of how to manage my mental processes in a healthy way.

There is another element for me in the answer to the above question. I like to be in control, and this could be one reason why I worry so much. Through showing others how much I care and am available, and somehow offering comfort, I achieve my goal of not thinking about my own life.

One thing I find most infuriating, when speaking publicly about my mental health problems, is the extraordinary number of people who think they can offer me a 'cure'. I get numerous messages saying something like, 'I was just like you, I took fish oils and it made me all better' – and other even more bizarre types of miracle cure. But then, I wonder how much I do the same thing to my friends. Advice from strangers can be annoying, but is it any less infuriating when it is from a friend? I tend to jump into my experience immediately – what helped me, my triggers, what is important to remember and how things might get better.

This is my way of trying to grab control, to fix things for them. But I know from experience that the best thing a friend can do is just listen to where you are at. While this is what I say to people who want to help a friend who is struggling but don't know how, often I ignore my own advice and try to offer solutions.

My desire to be in control, to feel that I can influence events and change things, also leads me to wonder how much I really trust in God to work in such situations. After a decade of illness, with prayers for healing unanswered (at least in the way I would hope for), I confess that this trust thing is a significant factor. If God won't answer my prayers for *me*, why would he answer my prayers for them? That is my logic, and it justifies my continued worry, as often there seems no hope of change. This is obviously exactly what everyone wants – a friend who has lost hope that their situation will improve!

It is all well and good to acknowledge the reasons why I absorb others' issues as my own: to distract myself from my life and its problems, and to feel in control partly because I have a limited trust in God doing anything to help. However, the real question now is: **What do I do about it?**

I can be pretty good at acknowledging my issues; it's resolving them that I struggle with. Being honest about my failings is easy, and is in fact entirely natural to my negatively programmed mind. In order to resolve an issue I need to change my approach to it and that challenge often seems thoroughly exhausting.

My counsellor recently suggested that I should try 'embracing my issues'. Rather than fighting the fact that I tend to absorb others' pain, why don't I accept it? If I can accept that this is a habit I lean towards, and recognize when I am doing it, then I can check on each occasion whether it is healthy concern or, more commonly, I am becoming immersed in other people's issues to distract me from myself.

This presents a gentler way of changing my approach to an issue. It is less about condemnation of negative cycles of thinking and more about self-acceptance and positive learning.

At this point I come back to boundaries. Essentially, I need to learn how to love others well – to empathize with them when it is appropriate, but not in an extreme way as a means to avoid dealing with the upheavals in my own life. I would also like to let go of the self-condemnation and shame that follows when I put such emotional boundaries in place. If I erect a boundary to protect myself and so enable me to love my friends well, by preventing me from worrying endlessly about them, my mind seems to take a giant leap to the conclusion that this is a demonstration of how little I care for them.

My mind seems to have things backwards. I tend to believe the lie that to show I truly love someone and am there for them, I should have no boundaries. The truth is, however, that in order to love my friends as they deserve, I need to have boundaries in place, otherwise I can never give them the best of me, and I will start to crumble under the impact of emotional 'stuff'. But I need to strike a balance, and not let my boundaries become walls that might prevent me from being involved in their lives and concerns.

My problems with emotional boundaries came to the fore a few years ago when I was living with someone whose refusal to respect boundaries led to a really toxic environment. She would leave for work early, and send me text messages on her way detailing some complaint, either with everyone in the house or with me specifically. This would be the first thing I read when I woke up, and it would put me in a funny mood for the day, because it meant that the day started with something angry. She continued with this habit even when I repeatedly asked her not to send these texts first thing in the morning.

This is just one example of how this person managed to get into my head and manipulate me. I had very few emotional boundaries and she was an expert at giving me guilt trips. It took a whole year after we had ceased contact with each other before I realized the extent to which I had been affected by this. Without any boundaries in place I caused myself a lot of damage, and was not able to develop a healthy relationship with her. The relationship ended in a way that was destructive for both of us, and just the prospect that I might ever accidentally bump into this person still causes me huge anxiety.

People approach their boundaries in different ways – how they implement and live with them – and I find this fascinating. Talking about boundaries leads to interesting debates and a good deal of temptation to judge folk (another issue I am working on . . .). One way that Dr Henry Cloud talks about boundaries is as the property line that goes around the home. It is clearly marked, but it doesn't have to be a wall. There is a gate through which we can welcome people in and let them go out. Over the years we may enlarge our property or shrink it down. The point is, it is up to us to establish and protect that line.

Consider the difference between a boundary and a wall. A wall is a permanent construct that is impenetrable. It is an aggressive statement. Boundaries should have an element of flexibility to them. We need to be open to consider their alteration, but we should not allow them to be constantly moved for us.

Biblically speaking, it seems to me that Jesus was the point at which the boundaries God had set up came down. However, Jesus clearly had personal boundaries that he kept to. For example, Luke 5.16 says, 'But Jesus often withdrew to lonely places and prayed,' showing that he was aware of his own needs and did not feel that he wanted people with him all the time. I am sure that his disciples might have been like, 'we can come too' on occasion, but he would take time alone when he needed to.

When trying to implement boundaries, I worry because I have had it done *to* me, where people have stated a boundary that felt like a rejection. Imagine you are going for tea with someone whose company you find draining. You could say something like: 'I am only going to stay for an hour. I have set myself a boundary that I should not spend longer than that with you as it drains me.' Or you could say: 'I have another appointment at four so will need to leave at three. How lovely to see you!' The first is about rejection, and protection of self at the cost of the other person. The second is about loving the other person while protecting yourself.

As with so much else in how Jesus lived, he set an example not only in words but in action. He needed time with his Father, so he prioritized it, but not at the cost of those he loved and those who loved him. He didn't hurt them to get it, he just acted.

This is crucial learning for me. I tend to go all one way or all the other – all in, or all out. Once I become too close and overwhelmed by a friend's problems, I retreat and sort of melt away into the background. Having been incredibly present for some time, I then suddenly disappear.

I know that living out healthy boundaries in my emotional response to the lives of those around me is about listening, praying, walking alongside and encouraging. It is also about ensuring that I set aside time when I won't be thinking about it or them – time that is solely focused on me and Mike and our lives.

I also know that it is not healthy, for me or my relationships, to seek to distract myself from my own struggles and to gain some idea of control through worrying about my friends' troubles. This often leads to me pulling back from people whose worries threaten to overwhelm me. I have a lot to learn about boundaries, and Jesus sets us a useful example. Implementing what I know to be helpful, though, can be a difficult next step. I have noticed that I have become more disciplined and made progress, and this is in part a reaction to being married. It helps to have someone to remind me from time to time that it is not my place to worry excessively about others. As I am an external processor, I find it is wonderful to be able to talk things through with someone who can question where I am coming from and point out when I seem to be getting obsessive.

I am also becoming less afraid of examining my own mind. I am digging deeper into who I am with less fear that the answer will be that I am an unlovable, unlikable loser. Examining my own state of mind has enabled me to be a better friend; I am not so likely to take on excess worry on behalf of others.

The truth is that carrying someone else's crap does not mean that they are not carrying it themselves. You cannot take the load from them and enable them to be worry free. Essentially, I am replicating what they are carrying and adding it to my own load. But trusting that my friends value me, and that I myself have value, has enabled me to talk openly and offer support where I can, without taking on their load.

I have been finding it easier recently to set my boundaries and manage them better too, having begun to accept the idea that I have something to offer people. I will chat with friends about their problems, and I will advise, comfort, encourage, or help practically, according to the situation. I will follow that up with a text, phone call or a cup of tea (this is not an exhaustive list of actions!) as regularly as I can. It seems so obvious really.

My boundary is essentially to be as good a friend as I am able without feeling pressure or obligation to fill my mind with their troubles. I worry and care, but can then put it down in order to focus on what is happening in my life and on my other relationships.

When written out like this it appears simple. Yet I have spent my life feeling that a good friend ought to worry about and focus on their friends' woes regardless of personal cost. Recognizing the fact that this is not healthy for me or my friends helps me to see that having boundaries in place enhances rather than detracts from how I am able to love those around me.

7 Numbers

The world of social media is fraught with issues when exploring your own self-worth. To me it seems to be essentially the outside world compressed. We often see, through it, the worst aspects of human nature; the nastiness we might use when talking about other people in the privacy of our homes is visible in a way that we have not been used to. The bullying that has always existed is now impossible to ignore. But there are good things too.

However, it is not the technology that is damaging to my self-worth, it is that all my insecurities are demonstrated in one small space, making them seem bigger and more prominent.

This chapter incorporates a little of everything I have spoken about so far. I use social media as a source of affirmation and to compare myself to others. It is easy within that world to avoid taking responsibility for our words, due to the ease with which you can throw them out into the ether. I also tend to find myself lost in the issues of those around me or in the depressing nature of the news.

Through this chapter I want to explore the impact of social media on my self-worth. Social media has been known both to boost my belief in my own worth and to destroy it. Through it I have seen the best of people and the worst.

I want to say here, that I really do *love* social media. I have become great friends with people I would not have met in any other situation. I am linked to a community of people who know what it's like living with long-term illness and understand the challenges faced by people whose bodies or minds are unco-operative when it comes to being healthy. I have found people who force me to see the world from a different perspective – I have been challenged theologically and politically, and have often had to rethink what I believe as I get a broader picture of the world from other people's viewpoints. Social media is also very useful for news gathering – depending on which news outlets you read, of course. I found a year or two ago that I was in the habit of only following left-wing outlets, so my news intake was becoming slightly skewed. I had to broaden my range to gain a more balanced view of what is going on in the world!

That aside, social media is a valuable source of information, a place for making friends and an opportunity to expand our understanding of the world.

However, one issue I struggle with that social media has raised for me is around numbers. For example, how many likes do I have, how many followers or friends, how many replies/comments on what I posted, and so on. It even applies to the opposite. I used to be very proud of how *few* friends I had on Facebook, because I only wanted to have friends who I really cared about.

The numbers game, and the affirmation it implies or denies, has at times occupied all my thoughts. Why did I suddenly lose 20 followers in one day? On that day I commented on my dog and his absurdly fluffy coat. Was talking about my dog not serious enough content for those followers?

I genuinely don't know what I would do if one day I found that everyone had suddenly unfollowed me. I think it would crush me, but I hate that I feel that way. It makes me angry! I don't want my self-worth to be based on the opinions of a bunch of strangers, especially as what they know of me is only what I have chosen to share with them.

It can be easy, with social media, to find value in what strangers think of us. We are offered a convenient plaster that can cover, with outside admiration, what we don't like about ourselves. It is the need for affirmation discussed in Chapter 3 magnified and intensified.

Before social media, more often than not we would seek affirmation from those we met through our day-to-day lives – work, friends, family and the extended circles created around these groups. You could show those people what you wanted them to see only up to a point, as some things are just impossible to hide from those who are around us, and from whom we seek affirm-ation. (I am aware, though, that some people excel at hiding themselves from people around them, but that is a whole other issue.) Now we can seek affirmation all we like, posting what we like to complete strangers or people we see once in a blue moon, with less risk of people knowing whether we are being fully truthful or not. We are free to gloss over the mess of our lives, present a perfect picture, and only those who know us well are able to challenge it.

Not everyone operates on social media like this, of course; many people use it to communicate with friends and family with no other motive than to keep others informed. However, while we rarely share the true picture of what our life is like, it is easy to believe that we know everything about someone based on what they share. The problem is as much in how we interpret the posts others put up as what we choose to put up ourselves. We can think from what we read that someone's life is going brilliantly well, when the reality may be that they are having an incredibly hard time.

By using social media we can often find a quick fix when we are doubting whether we are likable. We can post a happy family photo or an inspiring quote and be guaranteed 'numbers' that show we are valued – likes, comments and shares. This fix has a formula we need to follow to get the maximum impact. Let me explain.

A friend of mine, Sally, who is single, noticed that when a friend of hers posted on social media that she was in a new relationship, she immediately got countless likes and comments. What had she achieved? She had announced a romantic interest. Sally pointed out that there was nothing she could do that would garner as much response, unless it was to announce that she was in a relationship, engaged or having a baby. According to the social media hierarchy of affirmation, any other accomplishments pale in comparison to achievements such as these.

Soon after this conversation with Sally, I read an article that tackled this exact issue. A woman who had just got engaged felt that she was only now able to say what she had thought for years, but couldn't for fear of being called bitter – that getting engaged was not the greatest accomplishment of her life, despite what might be suggested by social media reaction. She did acknowledge that staying married for the rest of her life would be, but the engagement itself was not the pinnacle of her success.

The response we get to things we post on social media is conditional. People who get the most attention are those who seem to be talented and lead the perfect life. It is easy to manipulate social media to receive affirmation. Post what you know will gain attention. Announce a relationship, post loving family pictures or of yourself looking good, and go on exciting adventures – these will gain you more love and acceptance than anything else.

The online numbers game can mess with your head. When I have posted a tweet with a link to something, or a joke, and it has received zero response, in order to correct this or hide it I have deleted and rewritten it.

This is mortifying. Am I so desperate for people to tell me I am worthwhile that I will edit myself just to be acceptable? I have offline friends who love me, who read what I write, and who encourage me. But if I don't get a load of response to my blog, then really – was it worth writing?

The answer to this is yes. Writing helps me process and understand what is going on in my head. However, clearly my motivation for writing often becomes more about the response I receive than about what I actually write. And this means that I am likely to tailor what I write in order to get the best response – but as I have never been terribly good at doing that, it means that I may well just avoid writing altogether, to avoid the stress of wondering whether someone will like what I have written.

It seems to me that social media is essentially a battleground of value added and value detracted, and brings out both good and bad in us. It has undeniably added value to my life, but at the same time it has highlighted my fears and insecurities. The destructive and damaging side of social media can be huge, seen for example in the quick angry responses people throw out; it also makes bullying easy. A friend pointed out that with social media, while we have the option of 'not sending', the distance between us and our target can often dehumanize those we are being unfavourable about.

Once when I was in a Wahaca for lunch the comedian Russell Howard was sitting at the table next to me. This was in the days before my dad became the Archbish, so I had a very insignificant following. I tweeted, 'Russell Howard is sitting next to me in Wahaca. I don't know why I am so excited, I don't think he is that funny.' I didn't tag him, as it was meant to be a silly joke. He obviously wouldn't see it and I thought I was being funny. Anyway, Russell Howard went and favourited my tweet. I couldn't believe it and felt awful; this taught me a lot about thinking before I post.

But many people don't respond by letting others know that they have read unkind things said about them. It is easy to forget that everyone we talk about has feelings – whether we know them personally or only online.

There is a growing trend of bullying through others. People may share a tweet they have received that is unpleasant, perhaps from someone trolling them. They don't respond to it themselves, but allow their followers to do so. It leaves them looking as if they have reacted with grace and generosity, though the original troll can get a lot of abuse as a result.

This is a difficult area, because you naturally would like others to come to your defence if someone is unkind to you, and there is an argument that trolls deserve what they get. However, this seems to be passive aggressive behaviour; using our following to address unpleasant behaviour in others doesn't show us in our best light.

There is a flip-side to this. A friend told me that at one point someone had been particularly unkind towards her online.

She had been busy and had not checked her feed, but by the time she did so, the original unkind message had been deleted but her notifications were full of people defending her. Social media can offer wonderful things – people, often not anyone you know, can be ready to defend you, unasked and unlooked for.

On the other hand, social media can be damaging in the way we may use it to present our lives. If we hide what is really going on, this can isolate us and leave us struggling even more. For example, a friend of mine has been dealing with some marital issues – her husband is quite emotionally abusive. Yet to the outside world they have been happily married since the day they wed. They post happy pictures and loving words about each other; if you didn't know what was going on behind closed doors, it would be easy to assume that their life together is blissful.

Reasons for doing this type of thing can be complex. We may be unaware that we are doing it until challenged. For my friend, acknowledging that life is not going well, that married life is painful and not what she expected, is tantamount to saying she has failed. She is someone who finds comfort in others thinking she is 'doing well'. She gets a lot of likes for her photos, and many kind words in response to their declarations of love for each other. As a result she feels that she is succeeding in life. She doesn't see it as a lie, because she loves her husband; and she doesn't want to share the messy side of her life. Nor should she have to.

However, this means that she and her husband are protected from questions about the state of their marriage, because to the outside world it is obvious from their social media feeds that they are happy. They are, therefore, free from judgement, and free from accountability. No one can challenge her husband in relation to his bad behaviour, because no one will believe that it can be happening. In the seeking of affirmation for the success of their marriage they have protected their relationship from challenge, which has left her isolated and lacking the support that she needs.

This need for affirmation is strong and I am well aware that it is not just me who falls prey to it. My friend and her husband are not alone in regularly posting such online PDAs (public displays of affection). It is not something I have ever done – I consider them to be the online equivalent of sitting in a pub with a group of friends and snogging your other half. I figure, really, if you love them that much, just tell them face to face, rather than in a lovey-dovey post! You are surely communicating with each other through means other than social media alone?

My point is, I wonder who such posts are for. If it was for your other half alone, surely you would tell them in a more intimate setting? It strikes me that people have worked this out: if they post about their love and devotion or announce a significant change in their romantic or family life, they will get a huge response.

This judgement is not always fair, I know, and some people's motivation is good. When I was talking to a friend about the parent posts for Mother's Day and Father's Day, he said that the reason that he posted praise about his mother, even though she herself would never see it, was to honour her in front of his friends, and to acknowledge all she had done for him and given him. This conversation made me wonder whether I should do this for Mike. He has, in the years since we got married, been my carer – at times an almost full-time occupation. Should I be honouring him publicly for all he has done for me?

It is the motivation behind such posts that worries me. Perhaps this is me writing from my own insecurity – I often use social media for affirmation, so I assume that these people are doing it knowing that they will get a ton of love for such positive posts. However, if we regularly post only the best parts of our lives, and paint a rosy picture of a wonderful life and how everything is working out brilliantly, what happens when it all goes wrong?

My friend could end up trapped. If she starts telling people how tough life has actually been at home, they will wonder why she has been lying to them for years. If she acknowledges that her husband has been emotionally abusing her since they got married, she might not be believed, and might be accused of trying to hurt him and his career out of some sort of bitterness. What has been her defence mechanism, her way of coping with the challenges of life and the pressure to 'appear' to have it all together, could end up contributing towards a very difficult situation, where she is afraid to seek help.

The value added by social media – the opportunity to build networks, make friends, communicate with people you don't get to see very often – needs to be the primary reason for using it. If we use it as a way to fool those around us into believing that our lives are going better than they are or to get validation for how we are 'succeeding', this can turn out to be quite destructive.

The response to this is one often put forward by people who do not have the same love of social media as me. Come offline and live life in the real world. However, this completely ignores the positive aspects of social media: the affirmation (the healthy kind), the support networks, the fun, the news gathering. It is a simplistic response to a complex issue.

When I was very ill, social media offered me a route into the outside world that I couldn't get from 'real' life. If we threw out everything that can be used in negative ways and for negative reasons, we would never have progressed as a society as we have.

While I might not post in a lovey-dovey way about Mike on social media, the temptation remains to present a picture of myself and my life, to say the right things at the right times, things that will make others want to engage with me, to help me feel validated. My motivation here is skewed, because I would rather post things that I really want to, find interesting and want to share, rather than worry about whether others feel the same.

So what can I do to counter the impact that social media has on my self-worth? How can I ensure that when I do post something, I am doing so because it is something important or fun that I want to share, without needing to edit it to get the best 'response'?

In a similar vein to the chapter on affirmation, I guess it is about recognizing the unique value that I bring to the world. I have been working, through this book, on getting to a point of accepting that I do have value. However, what would the next step be? How do I take that acknowledgement of a baseline value and add to it?

In order to answer this, let's go back to the last chapter's question, and the favourite of my wonderful counsellor (my actual counsellor, that is – not God!): **What does this need for online affirmation give us?**

The simple answer is that it gives us a momentary release from wondering if we are acceptable to the world. But there is more to it than this. If I am told that I am valuable, at that moment I don't have to think about the value that I believe I lack. I can avoid dealing with my own insecurities for a little while (do you notice a theme here?). However, it is quite addictive: as with taking a drug, getting likes only means that you need more the next time in order to feel as good.

However, unlike in the affirmation chapter, where I talk about the struggle to accept compliments, I find that in an online context it is actually very easy to accept that others believe that I really do have value and that people mean what they say.

We have all seen that the internet can bring out the mean in people. We feel a freedom to say what we think when we don't know the person and are not face to face with them. The internet can provide a space for us to give 'honest' (often unfair) feedback. It is also the stomping ground of those who are very happy to inform you of your complete and utter worthlessness. This means that when a stranger says that I am good, I can believe that they actually think it is true. There is no relational investment encouraging them to say it so they must, surely, mean it.

This is what makes it so incredibly addictive. I don't always trust the people who love me when they compliment me – because they love me! They have a vested interest in making me happy (although, to be fair, Mike does tell me without fail when I am talking absolute rubbish – so I probably should trust him). I find it is easier to accept compliments from strangers you can't see, where your only connection is a small picture that often doesn't even show their face.

That, I suppose, is what I gain from online affirmation. But what about the numbers? I think it is the same thing. The compliment given is often just the like, or follow. If lots of people want to follow you, or like what you put out into the ether, this is a way of stating that you are important. It gives you a boost. The reason why losing all of that would hurt so much is that it would be a collective confirmation, essentially from the world, that you have no importance.

I was watching the film *The Help* the other day, and one of the maids, Aibileen, gives a little series of statements that she gets the girl in her care to repeat for herself – 'I am kind, I am smart, I am important'. This is what we forget, when we are so involved with social media. When we allow social media to run away with us and dictate our self-worth, it may tell us we are kind but only if others say so, we are smart only if others respond with approval, and we are important only if we have a blue tick.

I have fallen into the trap of believing that I am not smart and not important (I accept that I am, on occasion, kind) because my own value is so wrapped up in what strangers think of me that I cannot possibly believe it for myself unless others say it is true.

We have lost sight of the truth that we are all inherently important, we all have value, we are all 'smart' in some way (if not in the way the world values most) and we all have the capacity for kindness. Social media, with our drive to be accepted or heard on it, has led us increasingly to judge others based on a maximum of 140 characters, which in turn leads us to believe that if no one responds to what we post, we are being judged too. This is how my brain works, anyway.

In thinking about this I was reminded of Max Lucado's book *You Are Special*. It is about a town of wemmicks, which are wooden puppets. The main character is Punchinello, and Punchinello has a tough time of it. Wemmicks occupy their time going around sticking stars or dots on one another. Stars are given out when a wemmick accomplishes something – they can dance, or look nice, or have really smooth wood. Dots are given to wemmicks who are clumsy, or have rough bits of wood. But when a wemmick has a lot of either stars or dots, the other wemmicks will just carry on sticking them on, figuring that they must deserve it if they have so many already.

Poor Punchinello has loads of dots. He is embarrassed to go out and when he does he only hangs out with other wemmicks with lots of dots. One day he meets Lucia, who has no stickers on her at all. When people try to stick them on her they just fall off. Nothing sticks. Punchinello is amazed. He asks her why this is, and she says that she goes to see Eli every day.

Punchinello is scared, but wants to be like Lucia and so goes off to see Eli. Eli, it turns out, is the maker of the puppets. Eli is delighted to see Punchinello and tells him he is special. Punchinello says, 'Me, special? Why? I can't walk fast, I can't jump, my paint is peeling. Why do I matter to you?' Eli responds, 'Because you are mine. That is why you matter to me.' Punchinello is overwhelmed, and while most of his dots continue to stick, as a result of his visit to Eli one of them falls off.

This takes me back to the chapter on affirmation, in which I decided to accept that God knew me before I was born, that he created me and loves me for what I am. The story of the wemmicks captures perfectly what social media is for me. The whole town (many of them wemmicks Punchinello doesn't know) were involved in handing out praise and condemnation, and giving or keeping back affirmation, and everyone was complicit. However, they always needed or expected more from one another. If they had lots of stars they needed more stars; if they got lots of dots, they felt that they were worthless and a waste of space. It was through the relationship with Eli, the trusting that what he said was true, that the impact of the stars and dots started to lessen.

My need for and dependency on online affirmation, and the fear that comes from not getting it – or worse, getting criticism – stems from my core belief that I am not valuable. And if my value comes from others, I will never truly believe that I am valuable. The value that I believe myself to have has to come from within – and, as far as I can see, from two places: God and evidence. Like Punchinello, I have to start to believe that God truly does believe that I am special, even with my chipped paint and inability to jump. And I can find evidence from my day-to-day life to prove that I do have value. I can explore what I do, what people say to me, what I achieve and how I live and find things there that are proof of my value.

My dependency on the approval of strangers is harder to let go of, though, although I have recently begun to be able to do so. I don't monitor my numbers to the same degree any more, and I don't worry when a few people stop following me. I try to manage how often I check in online and make sure that I am balancing out the time spent online with that spent with those who love me offline.

Like Punchinello, all the dots that I believe are stuck on me will not drop off overnight, but I think that each time I acknowledge evidence pointing to the fact that I am valuable as I am, and each time I explore the promises God has made and the love he has shown me, another sticker falls off.

I really do believe that I am not only as valuable as the number of followers I have. I also truly believe that God sees what I am and is immensely pleased. This, right now, is enough to keep the stickers falling off, gradually.

8 Replay and regret

I touched on the idea of replay in Chapter 3: Affirmation. This is the constant replaying of particular conversations or social situations that lead me to believe I am inherently unlovable. I now want to explore this further, going deeper into the shame attached and the regular longing for the ground to swallow me up.

I can't remember when I last had a conversation with someone and didn't come out replaying the situation: what I said, how I said it, how it definitely offended the world, why I am not worth knowing and should never be in company again. This is particularly true if I don't get the chance to follow up or 'debrief' with them afterwards. It will have happened, but I wonder whether the event may have been so unremarkable, there wasn't enough of an opportunity to make a complete fool of myself.

Replay, and the subsequent regret, is a habit of mine, although I have become quite the expert at pretending that I don't hear the voice inside telling me that I have once again proved that I am a fool, an idiot or a bully. So, most of the time I can cope with these shame-filled replays; I figure that my mind is probably overanalysing (which is certainly true 90 per cent of the time) and I shrug it off. However, some situations create replays that become so epically toxic that they can paralyse me and completely derail relationships – not because someone has hurt me, but because I am so embarrassed and convinced that they think I am an idiot, that I will step back.

I am fortunate enough now to have friends who stick around, for all my quirks, and who are happy to challenge me when I do cross a line. However, this has not always been the case, and historically I have struggled to make friendships that last. My friends have often been people I really like, but the relationship quickly fizzles out and fades – in part, I am sure, to my own pulling back when I think I have put my foot in it.

I can easily jump on to my high horse in debates, and these are the most common situations that lead to relationship-challenging replays. However, just saying something incredibly stupid may have the same effect. My replay example in Chapter 3 concerned a heated conversation where I insulted the friends of a friend, and went on and on despite his clear discomfort. It wasn't done maliciously, and I was trying to fix it as I went along; I dug like my life depended on it until the hole was so deep I could barely see the light. Hence, a replay has lingered – blotting out my apology, his acceptance and an otherwise very pleasant evening, leaving me with a sense of shame every time I think about him.

Another replay of mine is quite similar. Although it happened about six years ago, it still haunts me with shame and embarrassment. It was a conversation over coffee with a friend, Jane, about reverse snobbery. I was doing my usual external processing, and voicing the thoughts that came into my head without thinking. We were discussing another friend, Mary, and saying that she had no idea how lucky she was. She was wealthy, though often complained about things that others would consider a blessing. She often treated me like I was from a different world.

We were both chatting calmly about the parts of us we didn't like so much, and then I got carried away talking about Mary, describing how she thought she was better than me, but in reality I was better than her. I did think about including here the conversation word for word, but honestly, you would probably burn the book and despise me. So in cowardly fashion I shall just say that I proved myself through the conversation with Jane to be an absolute snob and a rather unpleasant character.

Jane ended the conversation shortly afterwards, we got the bill and left and I haven't seen her since. In reality, I didn't actually think I was better than Mary. I was trying to talk about the absurdity of social hierarchy and 'good breeding', attempting to explain how I hated it that occasionally I also bought into the world that Mary lived in, and assumed a sense of being better than her. However, I explained this extremely ineptly; I was unpleasant about Mary and showed a side of myself that I despise.

I am not sure whether the fact that Jane and I have not met again is due to my utter embarrassment or her genuinely being put off by me oversharing aspects of me that I usually want to hide, and were an exaggeration anyway. Even after all this time, this replay fills me with enough dread that I cannot face recounting it in all its gory detail – and that's something I don't usually shy away from.

Compare this with another story from about three years ago. It was a media interview I was giving, and we were talking about my mental health. I said that I wished I was smarter, more intelligent, prettier. The interviewer stopped me, almost laughed and said incredulously, 'But surely you must see what you look like!' I felt utterly humiliated, because I had shared thoughts that were vulnerable and they had been brushed away as insignificant; or, more accurately, as if I had said this in order to fish for a compliment.

The interviewer then moved on and changed the subject. I didn't have a chance to respond to his disbelief that I should have body image issues. Every time I have thought about it (or seen the interview, which was shared on social media) I have felt that same, crushing shame.

However, this taught me something invaluable about halting replay. About a year after that interview happened, I was at the BBC, on a panel for the Time To Change mental health anti-stigma campaign, talking to journalists about how to interview people with mental health problems. I was there to talk about that interview and the harm it had done me. While the journalists were coming in, I saw the man who had interviewed me arrive. It was terrifying! Here I was intending to say how difficult that interview had been (for more reasons than that described above, but that was the primary one) and he was sitting right there!

It turned out to be redemptive, though. Throughout the event I felt the panic rising, and almost ran off stage about every 30 seconds. At the end I searched the room to find this poor man and apologize, and when I couldn't see him the shame I had started out with was quadrupled. Then he found me, and suggested we have a cup of tea and a chat.

He was sorry about the interview, because he remembered the moment I have described here. He had changed the subject abruptly because he knew he had gone too far. He apologized, I got to explain myself, and everything was rosy. Talking about it didn't delete my well-established replay immediately but it took the shame level down 95 per cent overnight, and within a few weeks it was gone.

It is very helpful to be able to contact someone after an encounter, if I know them well enough, to apologize and check I haven't caused any lasting damage. This is not the case the majority of the time, though, including both these examples. I couldn't get in touch afterwards to explain why I had said what I did, or how embarrassed I was.

However, the experience with the journalist showed me how important relationship is in dealing with replay and regret. I spent over a year revisiting that interview daily, feeling wretched and ashamed. Yet when we had had a conversation about it the replay sank back. It became a story rather than a source of shame. Unlike the example with Jane; whenever I think of her, I still feel embarrassed and small.

Having an opportunity to review is, I have found, essential to preventing replay taking root. I have a friend – who fortunately is actually a friend now – who I was so convinced hated me after our first meeting that I avoided her for two years. We had a conversation about the law the first time I met her. I was a police officer at the time, and her boyfriend was a defence lawyer. I had just come off a night shift, and though I don't think I was particularly unreasonable I was perhaps a little short, because I was tired. As this story is told from my perspective, however, I may just be making excuses!

Her boyfriend made clear his disdain for me and my response to this was, I believed, utter rudeness – a failing that warranted her wanting to be free from me for ever. I don't remember whether she actually said anything in the conversation. After that, every so often I would encounter her at social gatherings, and just hide away. I was convinced that his lack of 'like' for me would have put her off for good, even when I heard that they had broken up. Two years later, though, when we did finally hang out again, I learned that she had no recollection of the incident. My replay had been for nothing.

The reality of replay is that we allow one small thing to consume our thoughts – a word misspoken, an example misunderstood, that will often be overlooked by the other party. In our habit to make ourselves the centre of the world, it can dominate our thinking for months. This is what happens for me.

Recognizing the importance of checking in with friends after this type of replay-triggering conversation has been invaluable to me. It has got to the point that I will do this even after only a mild disagreement. A friend and I had a discussion recently about the Church and mental health (a common topic of mine). We had different experiences and therefore different approaches. The conclusion to the conversation went something like this:

> ME I will probably text you later to say sorry for over-sharing and being a bit rude.
>
> HER Oh, I do that too! I was just thinking I would do that when I got home.
>
> ME *You* were fine! It was a really helpful conversation but I think I was definitely rude so I am sorry!
>
> HER No! *You* were fine! I just misunderstood you!
>
> ME Oh dear. We seem to be the same. I will probably still text to say sorry.
>
> HER Me too. Bye!

Sometimes it is helpful that other people have the same issues as you. Sometimes it just highlights how silly they really are . . .

My counsellor often says, when I describe such encounters and detail how awful I was, that I am doing two things: letting someone live rent-free in my head, and deciding what people think for them – not giving them the opportunity to refute it.

In these huge replay situations – the shame-filled, never-ending, constantly remembering detail ones – the replay can control my thoughts for hours, days or weeks. I am therefore giving someone, without their realizing it, complete power over my thoughts. I spend all my time thinking about them and what they must think of me. They are living in my head without any check on what they are doing there.

This is not healthy for me, and it's not fair on them either. The majority of the time, the person concerned has no idea that I believe they think very little of me, nor that I am constantly obsessing over that fact. The idea that someone I like and respect might think that I hate them is awful – yet I regularly do it to other people. I take control over their thoughts of me and make them mine to decide. I wouldn't want someone deciding what I think for me, but I'm always doing it to others.

The truth is that nine times out of ten, when I speak to the person involved, what I'm sure they have been thinking has never occurred to them. The problem is that I rarely get to the point of having a conversation about it. I am more likely, as with Jane, to back away and avoid further interaction. The shame is too much, the embarrassment too acute; I just hope they will forget about me.

Occasionally, when such a conversation actually takes place, what I am sure that person thinks is confirmed. But then it is helpful to have it out in the open, so I can apologize. Unfortunately, the occasions where I get it right are rare, and are far outweighed by the times I have overexaggerated it in my head. I am convinced I am likely to be right, merely because I have been a few times before. I am rarely right, but those few times when I have been are more memorable than the gazillion times I got it wrong.

Whichever way these conversations go, the shame I feel after these encounters can be enough to cause me to want to avoid the other person for as long as I am able – usually until the shame has faded (which often means that the relationship has also faded) or our situations have changed to such a degree that I can recognize how much I overreacted.

The common theme through replay and subsequent regret is shame, and I want to explore this now. Perhaps by looking at the root of my always accessible shame tank I might be able to go through some of these encounters and come out the other side with a slightly more balanced perspective.

I was talking to someone the other day about the difference between guilt and shame. He said that guilt is felt when you have done something wrong. It is a 'right' feeling, in that it encourages you to reflect on what you have done and respond accordingly – with an apology and a change in behaviour. Guilt encourages us to develop better relationships through acknowledgement of wrongdoing. Shame, he said, is brought on not by our actions but by something more insidious. Shame encourages us to think less of ourselves, to hide away, to be less than we could be. It makes us believe in our worthlessness and uselessness and takes away our sense of self. It creates a hole, with no way out but down. His view was that guilt is brought on by God and shame brought on by the devil.

Guilt can be managed – if we respond to its prompting and apologize and make amends for whatever is causing it. Relationships can then be restored and the sense of wrongdoing ended. Shame, on the other hand, is unmanageable; it takes over our thinking, tainting and destroying relationships, leaving us no peace.

Since the clarifying conversation with the journalist who interviewed me, I have become more adept at checking my thoughts before replay can establish permanent roots that cannot be removed no matter how deep I dig. Talking about the problem made a world of difference to how that replay continued to play out. I have learnt that telling someone my suspicions of how truly awful I have been, and giving them the opportunity either to refute me or to point out where perhaps I need to apologize, means that replay doesn't have time to take root. Shame is dealt with before it can begin, usually by checking whether or not guilt is present. A text or phone call can make amends for any part of the conversation where I thought I went too far.

Shame, for me, can be hugely eased by a simple conversation and a recognition of a tendency towards it – though this feels awfully like treating the symptoms and not the cause. The question therefore becomes, why can I so easily be sent into a complete emotional spin by a conversation that may or may not have been slightly on the edge of polite, or showed me to be less than perfect? This question leads to the one I really want to address: **Where does this shame come from?**

This is a pretty big question, and I doubt I will be able to dig out all the roots, but perhaps I can unearth a few. If this is something you are dealing with, you might find it worthwhile trying to dig out some answers too.

The shame that I feel is based around my fears of what others think of me. This is where we come back to my belief that I need to perform, always be wonderful, in order for people to like me and stay around me.

I remember when I was in year seven and was just starting secondary school. I thought this might be my big chance to make an impression, to make lots of new friends, to be popular – not the usually quiet vicar's kid, who was occasionally boisterous and loud but only when no one but her friends were around to watch.

I got the opportunity to prove myself cool on the first 'non-uniform day'. I picked out my favourite top (to this day, I still love it). It was a yellow jersey rollneck, and what I loved most about it was the lines of little blue elephants holding one another's tails with their trunks going round it in stripes. With hindsight, for the mid-1990s I can see that this top was not 'cool' – though it was clearly distinctive. I got endless comments that day, and none of them kind, except one from a teacher (which doesn't count – you've hardly hit big time cool when a teacher compliments you on your outfit). Girls kept coming up and laughing, to my face, at my top. My favourite top.

Needless to say, I didn't become one of the cool, popular kids, but I did learn that what others think matters. I also learned that I don't have the ability to judge what is cool, and if I try I am likely to make a fool of myself.

It was made worse because we lived in a small town at the time, and everyone knew I was the vicar's daughter. I remember on one occasion using a swear word (this was when I was in year eight), and I got laughed at again. No one was impressed – I couldn't be cool and swear, because my father was the vicar! Although on this particular occasion, the girl who initiated the laughing was the daughter of a reader (a non-ordained vicar-type person), so pretty much the same as me.

These two incidents are both still on replay for me, and were sources of enormous shame for years. That shame has lessened as time has passed. I have learnt that swearing is not a demonstration of how cool you are. And honestly, I *loved* that top – I would gladly wear it now if I still had it and still fitted into it!

Moving house regularly only served to reinforce these types of lessons, as each school had its own version of cool. It is very hard to keep up with what you 'should' like or how you 'should' behave in order to fit in.

My point is that these incidents have had a lasting impact on me, teaching me that what others think of me is what matters. For the rest of my school career, on every non-uniform day I dressed in clothes as plain as I could. I only wore simple pale colours; eventually, in my late teens, I started wearing bolder colours, and only in my mid-twenties did I think of wearing patterns again – although never elephant stripes.

Of course, those girls who laughed at me had no idea of the impact their behaviour would have. I think that the shame attached to these and incidents like them has hugely affected how I view all my interactions. If I feel I have laughed at other people, or caused myself to be laughed at, I come away from the situation filled with shame and will replay the event over and over again.

Writing this chapter has highlighted for me how I behave. I do my share of laughing at others, and there is one friend in particular who I tease relentlessly. I have probably never had a conversation with him where I haven't teased him. I have always viewed this as harmless, but when I think back to my most shame-inducing moments, some have been when similar teasing has taken place with me.

It's not that we should never tease others, nor that people should not tease me, but we need to ensure that we laugh 'with' people more than 'at' them. The phrase 'sticks and stones may break my bones but words will never hurt me' is a lie. Words are so damaging; they cause intense hurt and shame, whether they come from someone about me, or come from me about someone else. Words can be extremely destructive.

The power of replay and regret lies in my perception of what others think of me; I cling to the words I have spoken or that have been spoken about me. The fact that this power has lessened in recent years is in large part due to the revelation of the value of relationship in tackling replays. Going forward, two things will help me to continue to deal with these issues.

1 Relationship – being aware of the need to be in relationship, to discuss replay before it takes hold, to apologize when I need to, to ask when I am not sure if I need to, and to gain reassurance when I think I have made a complete fool of myself.

2 Listening – something I am not so good at yet. Not listening in a debate is often the reason I come away shame-faced and replaying like my life depends on it. I get hot-headed, I *know* I am right and I *must* convince my opponent. Proverbs 18.13 says, 'To answer before listening – that is folly and shame.' So, in conversations, I am going to become a master of listening. No, really. Or at least I will try to be better at it, and to respond to people rather than get caught up in the debate and speak over them.

Finally, we come back to value. Being in relationship and listening may both mitigate the shame that might come up. However, it is through understanding our inherent value that we can prevent shame from becoming a problem in the first place.

I am tired of replay. I am bored of rehashing the same conversations and events over and over. I am exhausted by the shame that they bring me. I have two types of replays in particular, and I am working on ways of dealing with them.

First, there are the ones that need an apology – where I insult the friends of a friend, or tease a friend whenever I see him, or where I am rude or get all caught up in a debate and I am unkind. They fall into the category of 'guilt' and can be dealt with through relationship.

Second, there are the replays that come because I cannot believe I am good enough – where I am shamed by someone who does not know me expressing incredulity at my body image issues, or when I say something stupid that shows me to be less than perfect. These are the ones that come from perfectionism and a belief in my own inherent failing and lack of worth. With these, I need to look again at what the Bible says about my value. The Bible helps me to revisit the idea that I am worth knowing. I am acceptable, I have things worth saying and hearing, and I am, despite all that I am, lovable.

9 Major crisis, minor moment

Possibly my biggest issue is the need to be 'seen' as something. It runs as a common thread through everything, and this is something that has been clarified to me through the writing of this book. I need people to like me. While I've always been aware of this, it has been quite startling to realize that all the issues in this book essentially boil down to the fact that, without others affirming me, I am stuck believing the festering lies that I am unlovable, without value and useless. I am hoping that these beliefs will become less significant from now on, and that as I have thought through possible reasons for them and come to a place of greater understanding about myself, perhaps you will have done something similar, and also found a greater confidence in some aspect of who you are.

Here is another one for you, though – I am not quite done expounding my fears and insecurities. I have a terrible habit of taking some small experience, conversation or task I have been involved in and turning it into a monster. It is a bit like replay – going over and over a conversation and seeing it through the most negative lens possible – but doesn't last as long. It is usually resolved within a few hours or days and often results in me feeling a little foolish once I realize just how much I saw a mouse as a lion. The saying 'making a mountain out of a molehill' comes to mind.

This chapter is about my expectations, of myself and of others, and how I react when those expectations are not met. These expectations combine my lack of belief in my own inherent lovability with my perfectionism.

I have very high standards of myself; I wish I could do everything perfectly, and despite being aware that I can't, I get cross when I fail. I have an expectation that others eventually will decide I am not worth their time, and leave. These two expectations complement each other and present perfect opportunities for a major crisis to occur as a result of a seemingly minor occurrence.

Essentially, my identity is defined by what others think of me. When there is a risk that people will think less of me, I allow that to define who I am. While these 'major crises' are often resolved quickly and become little stories I tell in a self-deprecating manner to explain my excessive insecurities, I would rather not have the stories. They are triggered either by something said to me or by an error I make in a task I have set for myself.

I can turn a minor comment into proof that the person who said it doesn't like me or respect me. Obviously they don't need to be consulted about this, as frankly anyone in my position would come to the same conclusion as me. I remove the comment from the context of the relationship in which it occurs and re-define the entire relationship according to what I read into it.

A little while ago I received a text from a very close friend telling me that she was having a birthday party, which would be big, loud and full of people I didn't know. Now my friend is well aware that my anxiety can be triggered by being surrounded by lots of people, especially if it is noisy and people I don't know. A big party, away from home, full of strangers, is my exact recipe for an anxiety attack.

My friend suggested that instead of coming to the party, Mike and I could have dinner with her and her husband on a different day, just the four of us – a far more preferable option for my easily overwhelmed brain. However, my reaction to such a kind and carefully considered invitation was to decide that she didn't want me at her party, that she didn't really like me. I was her pity friend.

This led to several hours of complete despair. Of course she wouldn't want me at her party; I wouldn't want me there if I was her. How foolish of me to think that she loves me as much as I love her; she is obviously the superior being and far more likely to be loved than me.

All this from a simple text from a kind friend, recognizing that I wouldn't be able to enjoy her party, but wanting to celebrate with me all the same. When looked at objectively, setting aside a whole evening to spend with just me and Mike, as opposed to seeing us among a crowd, showed a significant amount of love. It meant we mattered! However, I could not understand that.

I texted back and tried not to sound upset, but she saw through it and called and we chatted about it. While I still felt unsettled, within a few days I was relieved, calm and feeling loved. My friend hadn't just said, 'I know this party will be hard for you, so if it is too much, please don't come, I don't want you to get stressed out.' She had actually offered an alternative way to celebrate, with a fixed date. She had acknowledged and accepted the whole of me – not just the version of me that is fun and easy to be around, but the me that is ill, and can be a bit reclusive. And

I took this as a rejection, rather than an overwhelming statement of care. I was upset because I had felt excluded and that maybe she wanted to hide me away.

I expect rejection and therefore I see it everywhere. This fear affects every relationship. A friend said to me the other day, 'It seems to me that you think that to be a "good" friend, you need to share everything and be told everything.' It was challenging. Do I really believe that? While the answer is a little more nuanced than that, it is, essentially, yes.

My friend raised this issue because I had panicked with her. She had asked me to hold her accountable for not talking with me about a big part of her life. While there were valid and sensible reasons for this, my insecurities went up and I thought that maybe I see her as a better friend than she sees me.

This is my constant belief. I love others more than they love me. Not in an 'I am so loving' sort of way, more 'I am unlovable'. It is a destructive way of thinking, and so relatively minor, and often loving, situations tend to turn into major crises.

I also make major crises out of my high expectations of myself. When I fail I think the world has disintegrated.

During my pregnancy I was almost entirely housebound. I would go out to see the doctor, and occasionally Mike and I would venture out to the cinema or to see friends, but those activities were conducted with an awareness of the impact they would have on me later. Pregnancy and chronic fatigue syndrome combined to keep me pretty much immobile. At home I could do very little; I could write for a bit, then my brain tired and I would need to rest for hours afterwards. Mike did all the cooking, and walked the dog. We have a cleaner who keeps the house looking presentable. I mostly just sat.

The point of this self-pitying information is to demonstrate how big a deal it was when I decided to make banana bread. I don't really like banana bread myself, but Mike does and we had some bananas that needed using up. So in a fit of energy I baked the bread. It was exhausting, but I felt proud. I was doing something kind for my husband. I was looking after him, admittedly in a tiny way, but I was doing something to show him I cared.

Anyway, when the banana bread came out of the oven, I left it to cool for a few minutes then I tipped the tin up. Here is when it all went wrong. It split into three parts: two broken pieces came out, but a third was left happily stuck in the tin. I completely fell apart. I started crying and ran out of the kitchen. Mike scraped the last bit out of the tin, put the pieces back together and left it all on the cooling rack.

I had a meltdown over banana bread. In my head all I could think was that I was the worst wife ever. Why had Mike married me? I was completely useless! I spent the evening and the following morning apologizing to Mike for being so rubbish. It was like my entire identity was tied into the success of that one baking venture.

I can understand why I reacted like that. I have been ill for most of our marriage and feel that I am a burden to him; I have never been able to do much for him. He serves me daily, looking after me gracefully and with much love. This was something I had saved up the energy to do for him, something that would show my appreciation for his care and kindness.

It was particularly frustrating because I can actually bake; I used to be quite good at it. Maybe this was just a tired over-reaction to my baking failure, but this wasn't the first time such a reaction had come about, and I haven't always had the excuse of pregnancy or chronic fatigue to justify the explosion. Something small happens, and I fall apart.

I don't know whether other people do the same – react like this over relatively small things. Perhaps it is an anxiety-related thing. If this sounds familiar to you, it might be worth taking a moment to consider why you react so explosively.

The question I want to ask is: **What would it take for you to feel secure enough in your relationships and actions to react rationally when the unexpected happens?**

I was talking to Mike after banana bread–gate and he suggested that perhaps, on that occasion, my identity was wrapped up in being a 'good wife'. It seems that I tie the whole of my identity into whatever I am doing and when it goes wrong I am left adrift, wondering who I am and what I am about.

This is true for both examples I have used. With my friend's birthday party, I struggle because I used to really enjoy parties. I would network and chat to anyone, I could make friends and have fun. I could blame how things are now on my anxiety, but honestly, I think I have just changed. I still love parties, and sporadically throw one, but then I remember they go on late and how tiring it is with loads of people and talking to them all . . .

As I have got more settled in myself I realize I am happier spending time with a few friends at a time; I am less ashamed of being an introvert. Parties always exhausted me, and now I just can't be bothered with the exhaustion and anxiety. I prefer being in a small group over a meal where you can go beyond small talk and have real conversations.

My friend's suggestion that I might cope better with a more intimate occasion rather than with a party challenged me to reconsider who I am. I had to assess whether I was still someone who wanted to go to a party. My identity was forced to catch up with my reality. I do not enjoy big parties any more. This may change if my health improves, or I may be a small groups kind of person for ever.

But this fact makes me panic, causing waves of self-doubt. Despite the fact that I don't feel the need to 'fit in' or be 'cool' as much as I did, I still can't help but think that those who are outgoing, 'cool', and who do parties well, are the people that everyone likes and remembers. Those who become an anxious bubbling mess are not worth knowing, and those who don't even want to go are frankly forgettable.

With banana bread-gate, there is a similar identity: the idea of being a 'good wife', or just a good baker. I became crushed under failure because I suddenly realized that I am neither. I then see all these marvellous cakes on Instagram (or similar) that people have baked – people who cook wonderful meals for their loved ones, who don't become a burden on them; everything is done in equal partnership, sharing tasks and responsibilities.

My desire to be liked by both friends and strangers is part of what sends me into a complete spin. My rational mind shuts down in a crisis and doesn't think logically about the fact that life changes and I cannot always be perfect. I shut out the fact that illness has become a regular part of my life and I am not up to achieving everything I used to do so easily. I react emotionally about the rejection I feel has been offered, or will be offered as a result of my failure, and about the fact that I will never be one of life's 'cool' people.

So I have established that once again this comes down to identity, which suggests that the way to become more rational in response to these sorts of events would be for me to change the way I think.

My counsellor says that we are not victims of our own brains, which tells me that change should be possible. If the way we think is unhelpful and counter-productive, then we need to change it. The question is how? She uses the example of living in a house that doesn't really work for your situation. There are three options: stay in the house as it is and do nothing; stay in the house but change what you can to make it better; or move house.

Applying this to changing how we think, the options become: stay in the negative situation as it is; stay in the situation but change it (and with this, you cannot change the other people who might be in it with you, only yourself); or walk away from the situation altogether.

As the situation I am talking about is how I think, walking away would be a challenge as I can't move away from my brain. However, if I am not a victim of my brain, then there are changes I can make; if I choose not to make them then I need to accept that my reactions and responses are likely to hurt myself and those around me, because I will continue to be unable to believe that people really are going to stick around.

I started by thinking about the ways in which it is commonly suggested you make changes. When you are focused on the negative things in your life, focus on the positive instead. However, the opposite of negative is not always positive. Focusing on the truth rather than on the positive can be more conducive to changing how we think.

Taking the baking incident, the positive was that the bread tasted good and Mike didn't leave me. The truth is that it wasn't the best banana bread, I did fail somewhat on that particular occasion, but Mike felt loved because I had tried. He enjoyed it and wouldn't leave me regardless of my lack of baking prowess.

The truth is often a balance of positive and negative, and can give us a clearer picture of how we operate and a sense of perspective. It also offers us a change if we want one. My banana bread-gate truth left me with a determination to make a better banana bread, which I did. It wasn't a huge improvement, and partly just involved being careful in extracting it from the tin. The truth can offer us an opportunity that positivity doesn't.

Positivity means that you think about only the good rather than the whole picture. The whole picture is rarely perfect, but is rarely all bad. I am not perfect, and therefore trying to be perfect is not going to result in my happiness and could have a negative impact on the happiness of those around me too.

Poor Mike not only had to take over the banana bread extraction, he then had to comfort his hysterical wife and spend hours reassuring her that he didn't think she was a failure or useless – rather than us both just giggling slightly at my failed attempt at a beautiful 'instagrammable' loaf and getting on with it.

Going back to my friend and her party, she had to spend half an hour on the phone assuring me of her affection for me and that she was just trying to help, when she had already done loads to show her love by offering a quiet dinner rather than a noisy party.

So, the next question I want to ponder is: **Is what you are thinking true?**

When you are wrapped up in your own brain it is very hard to get a perspective on this. I know for a fact that I am an utter failure and useless; however, I also know through experience that that thought is not true. I do fail, and there are certainly things I am useless at, but I also have strengths and value. We need to be aware of the lenses we might be looking through when thinking about things, and question how our insecurities and fears perhaps distort our thoughts.

Being an external processor, I find it incredibly useful having someone to talk things through with. This can raise its own problems; if you are desperately insecure and someone agrees that yes, you could have done something better, if you are anything like me you melt down. But it is still a helpful method of processing and establishing the level of truth.

If what I say as fact is declared by the other person to be a lie, then I need to reconsider how I think and question which declaration is true. For example:

ME I am a hopeless baker.

MIKE No, you have had many baking successes; just this one didn't work out as planned.

Is it true that I am a hopeless baker? Well, no, I have baked very successfully in my life. Therefore I must be OK sometimes. But I would be unlikely to get far on the *Great British Bake Off*. Finding the positive might help me to feel calmer about a situation, but finding the truth will help me to grow and become more comfortable with the reality rather than believe the lie.

This is really a combination issue. There is a lot of comparison in there (with people I follow on Instagram, for example) and perfectionism too (I am an utter failure at baking/going to parties). These two bouncing off each other is a bit of a disaster;

you can never be 'perfect' but it is even harder when you are constantly comparing yourself to others!

I am not as good as them and therefore I am 'the worst'. This is catastrophizing massively. And this has its own form of perfection. I need to be the best at failing to be perfect. It is an absurd and warped idea that prevents me from ever truly accepting other people's love and kindness, or allowing myself to actually acknowledge value in myself.

So we are back to the verse quoted in Chapter 1: 'But he said to me, "my grace is sufficient for you, for my power is made perfect in weakness"' (2 Corinthians 12.9). In the following verse Paul goes on to say, 'For when I am weak, then I am strong.'

This is what I always return to. My desire to be seen as perfect has a negative impact on me, on my relationships and on my relationship with God. It prevents me from allowing him fully into my life because it says that I don't need him; I am afraid of being weak, of failing, and that fear keeps me from acknowledging the full extent of my need for him.

God promises us that our weaknesses actually allow him room to work in and through us. When we acknowledge that we fail, we are weak, and we *need* his help, we become strong as he becomes a part of the story in an active and present way.

This verse is often quoted and it is one I have spoken to others about for years. Over the course of writing this book, I have thought deeply about what it means, and I have reached a point where I am slightly more content in owning and acknowledging my failings, insecurities and weaknesses. Not as a way to get sympathy, affirmation or help, but simply because that seems to be a more sensible way of operating.

This is not about putting yourself down, it is about knowing where your strengths lie and where the traps are that you tend to fall into. If we are able to say, 'I often blow small things out of proportion,' we can talk to those around us for a perspective that is not warped by our own fears, and we can pray about it. We can ask for God's strength in that place where we are so often weak.

This applies for all the issues I have spoken about, and many more. It offers God a chance to shine through us, but also to show us his very present and active love for us.

It won't mean that we immediately stop blowing small things out of proportion, or suddenly gain an alarming confidence in our own strengths. We are still on a journey to accept who we are. But this should allow us to go deeper into that relationship with God, from which strength, love and self-acceptance flow.

Epilogue: Finishing

My drive for perfection, my desire to be 'seen' and 'known', and my longing to be lovable – these things have dictated my life for as long as I can remember. The journey I have taken through writing this book is one that, a year into writing it, I thought had had no impact at all. I stopped working on the book when I was eight months' pregnant and picked it up again when my son was four months old. Reading it afresh after that break, I was disappointed. I felt I had not grown at all. Nothing had changed. All the issues I have written about are still a part of my life.

However, since coming back to it, in further writing and editing, I have come to realize that what has changed is my confidence. While I have made more progress in some areas than in others, I believe in myself in a way that I haven't before. The goal I set out with – to start to believe in my own inherent worth, to trust in the idea that I am in fact OK as I am – has not been met in its entirety, but I can see that progress has been made.

I recently gave an interview on the subject of shame. Will van der Hart was interviewing me, and asked me about my 'shame story'. In thinking about this question in advance, I realized that I have just written my shame story. This book is the story of my shame – what makes me feel that I am not worthy of love, or good enough to succeed. That made me think back to when I started writing, and consider again the progress I have made. I find that I have come a long way and I am proud of that.

The perfectionist in me is still strong, though, and as I come to the end of the book I can't help but panic. I am finishing what has been a big project, and for me finishing anything is an intimidating prospect.

I feel overwhelmed. There is the fear of what people will think of the end product. More than that, there is the fear of what *I* will think. Will I be happy with what I have done? Will I be willing to share it? Or will it fall into the hole of projects that never actually reach completion?

It's scary that something that has been so all-consuming for months will soon be over. What will I do then? I am hoping for a sense of relief that I no longer have to spend so much time thinking about what I don't like about me. But I can't help but wonder whether I will spend the rest of my life wishing I had taken this journey in private . . .

Finishing is a big deal. I don't tend to do it often. I like the start of a project, a new idea. As discussed earlier in the book, I have a habit of fantasizing a perfect end to anything I start, which leaves me with the impossible task of meeting those expectations. I like new ideas; I like plans and plots, and feel excited about the vast possibilities of what has not yet started, or is just taking shape. I am good at getting things going, and get carried away on the dream of something that could be brilliant and the idea of it coming to reality.

It's the follow-through I get stuck on. Very little in life seems to live up to the dream of what could be. After the hope and the fantasy comes the reality. The reality is the part I like to avoid.

This is particularly frustrating as there is something immensely satisfying about a project coming to an end. Having a host of loose ends, always having something to complete, is incredibly stressful. Just when I think I have caught up with my 'to do' list, for example, I remember a book I am halfway through reading, or another half-finished project.

There are many trivial examples of things I start but don't finish – painting by numbers, colouring in, TV shows – but they are just a reflection of the way my world seems to work. I get incredibly excited about the start of anything new, whether it is a friendship, a creative venture, even just a TV series – or something very significant, such as writing a book. I see the vision of how it will, or should, end. Then I assume that the reality will not match up. And the higher the stakes, and the greater the impact of not completing something, the more I am increasingly reluctant to finish.

When the going gets tough, I get out. Or I want to. The reality is usually that you can't pull out halfway through, and then my mental health starts to deteriorate. I get depressed, anxious and overwhelmed, and when the project is finally completed I am not able to fully enjoy the satisfaction it brings.

A while ago I worked on a project called the Mental Health Access Pack. It was designed to provide useful and meaningful information to churches and church leadership on mental health. It aimed to enable people like me to participate fully in church life, to feel welcomed and included; it would help leadership to recognize the damaging narratives that some people are hearing, and challenge them.

Having had both good and bad experiences within the Church, this cause was close to my heart and I cared deeply about the project, and still do. I want to see a healthy Church that is able to love and welcome those with mental health problems without fear or judgement.

The irony that this project sent my own mental health into a decline is not lost on me. I felt the pressure of everything I hoped it would accomplish, and overwhelmed by the prospect of it not working as we had hoped. In the end, it was completed, it worked well, and everything was fine. But I couldn't enjoy what had been accomplished. I was just glad I didn't have to think about it again!

It could be argued that this book is another symptom of my perfectionism playing out. I got stuck, here, at the very end. I didn't want to hand it over and have dragged my feet terribly. To seek encouragement, I went to the Bible to look for anything about finishing what you start, a bit of guidance in a godly kick up the arse kind of way.

The problem with my taking this route (to tackle anything, not just this) is that I rarely follow the advice the Bible gives me, unless I have thought it through and explored it in depth. It feels like I am just looking for a stick to beat myself with, when the truth is that that approach won't help me. I am more of a gentle encouragement type of girl.

There wasn't much there that would drive me to work harder anyway. But two passages did interest me. The first was Luke 14.28–30:

> Suppose one of you wants to build a tower. Won't you first sit down and estimate the cost to see if you have enough money to complete it? For if you lay the foundation and are not able to finish it, everyone who sees it will ridicule you, saying, 'This person began to build and wasn't able to finish.'

This is what I do. I am the fool who doesn't do the calculations before starting something. I just leap right in, without looking. I get carried away with ideas and don't actually think through the reality. This applies to almost everything I do – even my wedding. As my mum had to remind me the day after we got married, this really is what I wanted to happen!

I am certain I can do something at the start, then I begin to doubt, and when completion is in sight I panic. My confidence goes, and I either back away or get very depressed and scared, having to force myself to finish.

When Mike and I talked about having children, we worked it out carefully, considering my health and the wisdom of having a baby, speaking to medical experts, and to family, and so on. It wasn't until I got pregnant that I suddenly realized that the baby I was hoping for was *actually* coming. I was going to have to be a mum. Even then, as we got closer to the due date I thought a lot about the labour itself – but I didn't really dwell on the idea that there would be a baby at the end of it. That was far too scary. The fact that there was no turning back is probably the only reason I have a baby.

When he was born, they gave my son to me and I was stunned – in absolute shock. 'It's a baby! It's a baby! It's a baby!' was all I could say. Everyone laughed. What had I expected? But I had coped with 'having' to finish what I had started (by getting pregnant!) by just not thinking about life after completion (giving birth).

This applies to almost everything I have ever done. I go on instinct, then later spend ages wondering what I was thinking.

The second Bible quote I found that sort of addresses leaving things unfinished is Ecclesiastes 7.8: 'The end of a matter is better than its beginning, and patience is better than pride.' This is something I know, but rarely experience. I know that finishing something makes me feel good – if not straight away, eventually I feel proud of what I have done.

Essentially, then, I am a perfectionist who is afraid that the finished product will not live up to my expectations and hopes, and I leap before I look. I don't think things through and then I panic and try to back out. These are the reasons why I so often don't finish what I start. But here we are now at the end of something big. It will feel like such a failure if I don't finish this. In fact, pulling out now is practically impossible . . .

However, I have a problem with this book, which shows that despite having come a long way, through the writing process, I still have quite a journey ahead to get to the point of accepting myself as I am. Despite finishing the book, in terms of writing, I haven't actually finished it. It isn't really concluded. I can't walk away from it and say, 'Ta-da! Look how wonderful I am!' I don't feel that I am wonderful at all.

I am aware that many of the chapters end with an unspoken 'but'. They often conclude that there are things I need to accept about myself and states of mind that I aspire to. It doesn't feel finished, but that is sort of the point.

Before I wrote this book I really didn't like who I was. I have finished the book less critical of myself and more accepting. The issues I have written about seem to be familiar to many people I speak to. I still compare myself to those around me, I still look to place blame for my bad behaviour on others, but my acceptance of not being perfect is significantly higher than it was, and my need for affirmation through social media is diminishing.

I wanted to make my journey in the hope that it would help others journey too. You may have come to the end of it wondering, like me, if it has really made any difference to how you feel about yourself. Chances are it has made a difference, not because of my magical writing skills, but because through thinking about the issues that tie us down, we can start to loosen the knots. There is no quick fix to make us happy and self-accepting, humble and generous, kind, and whatever else you wish you were. But that is what makes life interesting.

There will always be people who can demonstrate, if you allow them to, how you are not living life right. Just after Mike and I got married I read one of those silly articles that explains what your sleeping position says about your relationship. Because we sleep back to back in bed, apparently our marriage is doomed to fail. A small and insignificant example, but initially I did worry, as I am prone to do. Does this suggest a lack of intimacy? Should we cuddle more? Is that the way to a lasting marriage? Then I stopped myself. I decided this article was absurd, and how Mike and I sleep is unlikely to cause the collapse of our marriage. I am happy with that conclusion. The oversimplification of life leads us to believe that there is only one way to live well, to be a success, to be loved. Which, honestly, is nonsense.

So, I come to the end of this book afraid to finish, but excited to have completed it. More confident that I am loved, I have value; I am talented in my own way, and different from others, and that is OK. I am more settled into the idea of trusting that God created me for a purpose, and that I don't need all the information on what that purpose is right now.

I am finishing this book, and I hope you have gained something through it. Grown-up life hasn't turned out quite how I expected, and while I wish that I could just have the cake part of life, I accept that carrots are sometimes healthier, on occasion more interesting and possibly even exciting. Proper grown-upping is really hard, and I just wish . . .

JOKES! I planned to end on a half-finished sentence, but then I realized, I can't. I am still battling the perfectionist in me.

Bibliography

David Benner, *The Gift of Being Yourself: The sacred call to self-discovery*, Downers Grove, IL: InterVarsity Press, 2015.

Brené Brown, *The Gifts of Imperfection*, Center City, MN: Hazelden, 2010.

Mary Burgess with Trudie Chalder, *Overcoming Chronic Fatigue: A self-help guide using CBT*, London: Robinson, 2005.

Henry Cloud, *Changes That Heal*, Grand Rapids, MI: Zondervan, 1992.

Will van der Hart and Rob Waller, *The Perfectionism Book*, London: Inter-Varsity Press, 2016.

Max Lucado, *You Are Special*, Oxford: Candle Books, 2004.

Marianne Williamson, *A Return to Love*, London: HarperCollins, 1992.